Donburi

DELIGHTFUL JAPANESE MEALS IN A BOWL

Donburi

DELIGHTFUL JAPANESE MEALS IN A BOWL

AKI WATANABE

Marshall Cavendish
Cuisine

To my parents,

Katsushi and Fumiyo Watanabe

Photographer: Liu Hongde, Hongde Photography

Copyright © 2014 Marshall Cavendish International (Asia) Private Limited

First published 2014
This new edition 2022

Published by Marshall Cavendish Cuisine
An imprint of Marshall Cavendish International

 A member of the
Times Publishing Group

Other Marshall Cavendish Offices:
Marshall Cavendish Corporation, 800 Westchester Ave, Suite N-641, Rye Brook,
NY 10573, USA • Marshall Cavendish International (Thailand) Co Ltd, 253 Asoke,
16th Floor, Sukhumvit 21 Road, Klongtoey Nua, Wattana, Bangkok 10110, Thailand
• Marshall Cavendish (Malaysia) Sdn Bhd, Times Subang, Lot 46, Subang Hi-Tech
Industrial Park, Batu Tiga, 40000 Shah Alam, Selangor Darul Ehsan, Malaysia

Marshall Cavendish is a registered trademark of Times Publishing Limited

Printed in Singapore

CONTENTS

ACKNOWLEDGEMENTS

I would like to express my gratitude and appreciation to all who contributed in no small part towards the publication of this book.

First and foremost, I would like to thank Lydia Leong, who gave me the opportunity to work with a fabulous team at Marshall Cavendish. Also, a big heartfelt thank you to the editor, Audrey Yow, for providing guidance and allowing flexibility in the content presentation for this book. Special thanks to Liu Hongde for the beautiful photography and to Lynn Chin for providing art direction. This is an incredibly professional team that helped create something we can all be proud of.

Special thanks also go to Kikkoman Singapore Pte Ltd and Tawaraya Singapore, who rendered invaluable assistance by supplying the best ingredients for the photoshoot. I would also like to thank Mrs Junko Harris for helping to translate some of the texts from Japanese to English.

I must thank the people I met during this incredible journey in Singapore, who helped me get to where I am today. To Ms Shermay Lee and the staff at Shermay's Cooking School, thank you for all the assistance and encouragement you have been giving me since I joined the team. It has been an enriching and fulfilling experience for me to share the art of Japanese cuisine at this school.

To all my students, it has been great pleasure to be able to share what I know with you. I also gained invaluable experience from all of you through bantering in class and other interactions. Thank you for your warmth, patience and encouragement.

And to my husband, Leroy Ahino, the meat-eater, thank you for being my food taster and critic.

Finally, thank you for picking up this book. Food is wonderful, but when prepared for someone you care about, it becomes even more special. Cooking for a loved one is a means of conveying your love and appreciation. In a way, this book is like a collection of love letters. I do hope that these recipes make wonderful love letters to that special person, whether you are trying these recipes for someone or giving this book to a person that you care about.

INTRODUCTION

Donburi originally refers to a deep bowl, which can be made from wood, ceramic or clay. These bowls come in various patterns, and may have a cover. Today, *donburi*, *donburi-mono* (*don-mono* in short) or *don* are used to mean a rice meal topped with any ingredient. In a broad sense, cooked rice in a lunchbox topped with ingredients is also called *donburi*. Even non-Japanese food served in this manner is considered a *donburi*.

This Japanese concept dates back to the Edo period (1600s to late 1800s). As it was tasty, nutritious and easy to prepare, it became popular, with people trying various ingredients to go with the rice.

This book contains 50 *donburi* recipes, most of which can be prepared within 30 minutes. They make very hearty and satisfying meals, and can be served with a simple salad or soup if you like.

Generally, *donburi* toppings have stronger flavours and may have a little more liquid if not served on top of rice. The recipes in this book use 200 g (7 oz) steamed rice per serving. Try them and adjust the rice amount according to your preference.

It will be my greatest pleasure if these recipes become part of your collection for great home-cooked meals.

Aki Watanabe

Quick and Easy

Beef and Cabbage French Mustard Don
Gyuniku to Cabetsu no Mastard Shoyu Don

Tangy Dijon mustard and savoury soy sauce compliment the sweet fragrance of beef. This delicious mix of eastern and western flavours goes very well with steaming white rice.

SERVES 2

Beef chips 140 g (5 oz), thinly sliced
Koikuchi soy sauce 1 tsp
Sake 1 tsp
Celery 50 g (1²/₃ oz)
Canola oil for stir-frying
Beijing cabbage about 4 leaves, cut into 3-cm (1¹/₄-in) squares
Steamed rice 400 g (14 oz)
Chopped spring onions (scallions) for garnishing
SEASONING
Koikuchi soy sauce 2 Tbsp
Dijon wholegrain mustard 2 tsp–1 Tbsp
Mirin ¹/₂ Tbsp

1. Marinate beef with 1 tsp koikuchi soy sauce and sake for 5 minutes.

2. De-string celery and slice diagonally.

3. Mix seasoning ingredients together. Set aside.

4. Heat oil in a pan. Stir-fry beef until it partially browns. Mix in seasoning.

5. Add celery and stir-fry briefly before adding Beijing cabbage. Cook until cabbage softens.

6. Serve on rice and garnish with spring onions.

Note: Adjust amount of Dijon mustard according to taste.

Stir-fried Pork and Kimchi Don
Buta Kimchi Don

This Korean-flavoured dish is commonly served in an *izakaya*, a Japanese-style tavern. Spicy *kimchi*, a kind of fermented pickled vegetable from Korea, blends very well with other fermented ingredients like soy sauce and cheese.

Korean spicy bean paste (*gochujang*) 25 g (⁴/₅ oz) + more if desired

Sake 2 tsp

Johakuto sugar ¹/₂ tsp

Koikuchi soy sauce 1 tsp

Sesame oil for stir-frying

Sliced pork belly 150 g (5¹/₃ oz), cut into 3-cm (1¹/₄-in) strips

Yellow onion 1 heaped Tbsp, peeled and grated

Garlic 1 clove, peeled and grated

Cabbage *kimchi* 100 g (3¹/₂ oz)

Chinese chives (*ku chye*) 75 g (2²/₃ oz), ends trimmed and cut into 4-cm (1³/₄-in) lengths

Bean sprouts 100 g (3¹/₂ oz), washed and heads removed

Salt to taste

Ground black pepper to taste

Pizza cheese 30 g (1 oz)

Steamed rice 400 g (14 oz)

1. Mix Korean spicy bean paste, sake, sugar and koikuchi soy sauce in a bowl. Set aside.

2. Heat sesame oil in a pan over medium-high heat. Stir-fry pork belly until it browns.

3. Add yellow onion and garlic. Fry until fragrant.

4. Add *kimchi* and fry for 1 minute.

5. Add chives and bean sprouts. Season with salt and pepper if desired. Sprinkle pizza cheese over.

6. Serve on rice. Top with pepper and add more Korean spicy bean paste if desired.

Pork Belly with Shiso Butter Soy Sauce
Buta no Shiso Butter Don

SERVES 2

Shiso leaves 12

Canola oil 1 tsp

Pork belly steak 250 g (9 oz),
  sliced into 5-cm (2-in) strips

Unsalted butter 15 g (1/2 oz)

Koikuchi soy sauce 1 1/2 Tbsp

Mirin 3 Tbsp

Steamed rice 400 g (14 oz)

Sweet pork belly and rich butter with the refreshing flavour of shiso leaves create an appetising fragrance.

1. Finely shred shiso leaves. Set half of the shredded shiso aside for garnishing.

2. Heat oil in a frying pan. Pan-fry pork belly on both sides. Remove from heat when browned. If pan is sticky, wipe with a paper towel.

3. Heat butter, koikuchi soy sauce and mirin in the pan. Add pork and shredded shiso leaves to glaze. Note that shiso will blacken when glazed. Reserve sauce for drizzling later.

4. Arrange glazed shiso over pork on rice. Drizzle sauce over. Garnish with shredded shiso and serve.

Japanese Curry Don
Kare Don

SERVES 2

Japanese curry is great with *udon*, a type of white wheat noodles, too. Use vegetables of your choice, such as spinach, yellow onion or carrot.

Shiitake mushrooms 6

Japanese leek 1 stalk

Deep-fried bean curd puff (*aburaage*) $^1/_2$ piece

Canola oil 1 Tbsp

Pork belly 200 g (7 oz), sliced into 4-cm (1$^3/_4$-in) lengths

Japanese curry powder 1 tsp

Japanese stock (*dashi*) 500 ml (16 fl oz / 2 cups)

Mirin 1 Tbsp

Koikuchi soy sauce 1 Tbsp

Instant curry cube 40 g (1$^1/_3$ oz)

Potato starch 1$^1/_2$ Tbsp

Water 3 Tbsp

Steamed rice 400 g (14 oz)

Chopped spring onions (scallions) for garnishing

Pickles as side dish

1. Remove stems from mushrooms. Wipe mushrooms with a damp paper towel and slice into 1 cm ($^1/_2$ in) thick pieces.

2. Taking only the white part of the leek, slice diagonally into 1-cm ($^1/_2$-in) lengths.

3. Blanch bean curd puff briefly and cut into 3-cm (1$^1/_4$-in) strips.

4. Heat oil in a pot. Stir-fry pork belly over medium-high heat until it browns. Add mushrooms, aburaage and leek. Stir-fry for 2 minutes. Add curry powder and stir.

5. Add stock, mirin and koikuchi soy sauce. Bring to a boil. Add curry cube and allow it to melt.

6. Mix potato starch and water together. Stir into the pot to thicken the mixture.

7. Pour curry onto rice. Top with spring onions and serve with pickles at the side.

Miso

Miso is an essential seasoning in Japanese cuisine. From soups to stews or stir-fries, it can be used as a seasoning or marinade. In Japan, there are over 1,500 kinds of miso from various regions. To accommodate my father's job and my school transfers, our family moved several times across the east and west of Japan.

Miso was the first ingredient I noticed tasted different across different regions. Our family used salty brown miso from Tokyo, where my grandmother was from. I was surprised to find that the taste of miso became sweeter as we went westward.

Miso is a paste of fermented soy beans with salt and *koji*, a type of fungus made from rice, barley or soy beans. Its taste depends on the type and amount of *koji* used, and how long it has been fermented. There are various kinds of miso available, so it will be useful to know the three basic kinds of miso before you make your purchase. In terms of appearance, they come in dark brown, medium-brown or light-coloured shades. The lighter-coloured the miso, the shorter the fermentation time and the lower the salt content. Here are the alternative miso names: dark brown miso = red (*aka*) miso, medium-brown miso = light-coloured (*tanshoku*) miso, light-coloured miso = white (*shiro*) miso. Miso continues to ferment as time goes by, and the colour will turn darker. To slow down the fermentation process, cover miso with cling film and refrigerate it to minimise contact with outside air.

There are three types of miso used in this book. The first is shinshu miso, which ranges from light to reddish brown, and is a little high in salt. While shinshu miso is usually used for soups, it can also be used for other dishes. Next is hatcho miso, which is highly salted and slightly sour, and comes in dark red or dark brown colours. Lastly, saikyo miso is sweet white miso, which is used in the Kyoto region for both sweet snacks and savoury food.

I sometimes mix different types of miso to produce the desired taste. Miso can be eaten raw, so you can try mixing different types of miso and tasting it before adding to your food. Note that when using miso for warm dishes like soups or stir-fries, it is important to minimise the cooking time after adding miso so that its flavour is not lost.

Pork Liver and Chinese Chives Don
Leba Nira Don

Pork liver is a good source of iron and vitamin B, ideal for those suffering from anaemia or fatigue. Choose pork liver that is fresh and bright red.

SERVES 2

Sesame oil for stir-frying + 2 tsp for seasoning

Chilli bean paste 2 tsp

Onion 70 g (2^1/$_2$ oz), peeled and sliced

Garlic 1 tsp, peeled and grated

Chinese chives (*ku chye*) 150 g (5^1/$_3$ oz), cut into 4-cm (1^3/$_4$-in) lengths

Bean sprouts 100 g (3^1/$_2$ oz), washed and drained, heads and tails removed

Red chilli slices (optional) to taste

Potato starch 1 tsp + 1 Tbsp water

Ground black pepper to taste

Steamed rice 400 g (14 oz)

SEASONED PORK LIVER

Pork liver 200 g (7 oz), thinly sliced

Milk enough to cover pork liver slices

Koikuchi soy sauce 2 tsp

Sake 2 tsp

SAUCE

Sake 20 ml (²/₃ fl oz)

Koikuchi soy sauce 20 ml (²/₃ fl oz)

Johakuto sugar 2 tsp

Grain vinegar (*kokumotsu su*) 2 tsp

Oyster sauce 1 Tbsp + 1 tsp

1. Prepare seasoned pork liver. Soak pork liver in milk for 10 minutes. Drain and pat dry with a paper towel. Season with koikuchi soy sauce and sake for 5 minutes.

2. Mix sauce ingredients together in a bowl. Set aside.

3. Heat oil in a pan over medium heat. Stir-fry pork liver for 1 minute. Add chilli bean paste and fry briefly. Remove from heat and set aside.

4. Add onion and garlic. Stir-fry onion until semi-translucent, then add chives and bean sprouts. To add more spice, add red chilli slices at this point with chives and bean sprouts. Stir-fry briefly.

5. Return pork liver to the pan and stir to mix, then add sauce.

6. Stir in potato starch and water mixture quickly, then season with 2 tsp sesame oil, followed by pepper.

7. Serve on rice.

Spicy Prawn Don
Ebi Chilli Don

Ebi is a Japanese word for "prawn" or "shrimp". This is one of my elder sister's favourite dishes. She always requested to order this dish whenever we dined out in Chinese eateries. A simple treat of stir-fried prawns seasoned with tomato sauce and spicy chilli bean paste, this can definitely win over a child, just as it did with my sister.

SERVES 2

Tiger prawns 20–24

Canola oil for stir-frying

Yellow onion ¼ head, peeled and finely chopped

Garlic ½ tsp, peeled and chopped

Ginger ¼ tsp, peeled and chopped

Chilli bean paste 2 tsp

Steamed rice 400 g (14 oz)

Sliced spring onions (scallions) for garnishing

MARINADE

Egg white 1 Tbsp

Potato starch 1 tsp

Canola oil 1 tsp

Bicarbonate of soda a pinch

Salt a pinch

Ground white pepper a pinch

SEASONING

Chicken bones soup granules ⅛ tsp

Water 2 Tbsp

Tomato ketchup 2 Tbsp

Johakuto sugar 1 tsp

Koikuchi soy sauce 2 tsp

1. Shell prawns and remove the heads, leaving the tails intact. With a knife, make slits along the back of each prawn to remove the vein.

2. Stir to mix marinade ingredients in a bowl. Add in prawns to marinate. Let it stand for 15 minutes.

3. Bring a pot of water to a boil. Drop in prawns and cook for 30 seconds. Drain and set aside.

4. Stir to mix seasoning ingredients in a bowl. Set aside.

5. Heat oil in a pan or wok. Stir-fry onion until half translucent, then add garlic and ginger. Fry until fragrant. Add spicy chilli bean paste and stir briefly. Add prawns and seasoning ingredients. Stir to coat prawns. Remove from heat once prawns are cooked through. Do not cook for too long or the prawns will become dry.

6. Serve on rice. Garnish with spring onions and serve.

Tofu and Mushroom Don
Tofu Kinoko Don

Silken tofu 300 g (10½ oz)

Mixed mushrooms (e.g. shimeji, enoki, shiitake or oyster mushrooms) 150 g (5⅓ oz)

Japanese stock (*dashi*) 250 ml (8 fl oz / 1 cup)

Koikuchi soy sauce 40 ml (1⅖ fl oz)

Mirin 50 ml (1⅔ fl oz)

Old ginger 1 tsp + more for garnishing, peeled and grated

Potato starch 1 tsp + 1 Tbsp water

Steamed rice 400 g (14 oz)

Shredded Japanese leek for garnishing

This is a light homely meal that is both tasty and healthy. If you do not feel like taking protein from meat, try this.

1. Pat dry tofu with paper towels and cut into bite-size pieces.

2. Slice mushrooms into bite-size pieces. If using shiitake mushrooms, remove the stems and wipe the surface clean with a damp paper towel.

3. In a pan, bring stock, koikuchi soy sauce and mirin to a boil. Add mushrooms and tofu. Lower to a simmer for 10 minutes, until tofu has browned.

4. Add ginger and turn up the heat. Stir in potato starch and water mixture to thicken.

5. Serve on rice, then garnish with leek and ginger.

Shabu-shabu Pork with Umeboshi and Sesame Sauce Don
Butashabu Ume Goma Don

Umeboshi are preserved plums with a sour and salty taste. It is commonly used to cook fish or served as a filling for *onigiri* (Japanese rice balls). The refreshing combination of tangy umeboshi and sweet pork makes a wonderful salad-style don for a hot day.

SERVES 2

Shabu-shabu pork slices 200 g (7 oz)
Shiso leaves 4
Yellow onion 1/2 head, peeled
Japanese cucumber 1/2
Steamed rice 400 g (14 oz)
Toasted white sesame seeds (*iri goma*) 1 tsp
UMEBOSHI AND SESAME SAUCE
Umeboshi 3 tsp, de-seeded and chopped
Toasted white sesame seeds (*iri goma*) 3 Tbsp, ground
Sesame oil 3 Tbsp
Honey 2/3–1 tsp
Mirin 2/3–1 tsp
Usukuchi soy sauce 2 tsp
Japanese stock (*dashi*) 4 Tbsp
Fine bonito flakes (*katsuobushi*) 3 Tbsp
White sesame paste (*neri goma*) 1 Tbsp

1. Briefly blanch pork slices in simmering water one at a time. Plunge into iced water to prevent over-cooking. Drain and pat dry with paper towels.

2. Finely shred shiso leaves. Soak in water for 1 minute. Drain and pat dry with paper towels. Set aside.

3. Slice onion thinly. Soak in water for 10 minutes and drain.

4. Shred cucumber and mix with sliced onion. Chill in the refrigerator until needed.

5. Combine all ingredients for umeboshi and sesame sauce. Stir until very well mixed.

6. Scatter onion and cucumber mix over rice. Top with pork slices and sprinkle sesame seeds over.

7. Garnish with shredded shiso leaves. Serve with umeboshi and sesame sauce.

Bonito Flakes

Bonito flakes, or *katsuobushi*, are used in many ways for Japanese food. It is commonly used as garnishing and as a basic ingredient for Japanese fish stock (*dashi*). These flakes come from the bonito fish, which are filleted and then smoked several times.

The fillets will then be dried and matured before they are shaven into flakes. In the past, people used to keep a big chunk of bonito fillets at home, which they shaved when needed. Today, people usually buy shaved bonito flakes from the supermarket.

Depending on what you need it for, bonito flakes come in different sizes. Coarser flakes are good for preparing stock, and finer ones serve better as a topping.

As bonito flakes oxidise quickly, it is best to use them up as soon as possible after opening and keep them refrigerated.

Natto Vegetable Don
Neba Neba Don

Natto, or fermented soy beans, have a strong smell and slimy texture. It is commonly served as it is or with raw egg and soy sauce for breakfast. As with durian, you either love it or hate it. I love natto and sometimes have a strong craving for it. Natto is nutritious and it doesn't require cooking, so it is a very convenient and healthy food choice.

SERVES 2

Koikuchi soy sauce 2 Tbsp
Sake 1 Tbsp
Mirin 2 Tbsp
Bonito flakes (*katsuobushi*) 6 Tbsp
Natto 100 g (3¹/₂ oz)
Japanese mustard (*karashi*) (optional) ¹/₈ tsp
Lady's fingers (okra) 4
Japanese yam (*nagaimo / huai san*) 200 g (7 oz), peeled
Fresh egg yolks for raw consumption 2
Steamed rice 400 g (14 oz), at room temperature
Shredded nori seaweed (*kizaminori*) to taste

1. Prepare sauce. Heat koikuchi soy sauce, sake and mirin in a pan. When it comes to a boil, add bonito flakes and simmer for 30 seconds. Strain and leave to cool to room temperature before chilling in the refrigerator until needed.

2. Stir natto with chopsticks until it becomes foamy and more sticky. Add Japanese mustard and mix well.

3. Boil water in a pot with a pinch of salt. Boil lady's fingers until cooked. Drain and plunge into iced water. Strain and set aside to cool before slicing thinly.

4. Grate Japanese yam and mix with lady's fingers. Mix with half of the chilled sauce. Stir well and spread over rice.

5. Top with natto and a raw egg yolk for each serving.

6. Serve with shredded nori seaweed and remaining sauce if desired. This is best eaten with all ingredients mixed together.

Spicy Cod Roe and
White Radish Sprouts Don
Karashi Mentaiko Kaiware Daikon Don

SERVES 2

Spicy cod roe (*karashi mentaiko*) 1 sac,
 about 60 g (2 oz)

Extra virgin olive oil 4 tsp

Fresh lemon juice 1/4 tsp

Salt-preserved seaweed (wakame)
 20 g (2/3 oz)

Steamed rice 400 g (14 oz), at room
 temperature

Toasted white sesame seeds (*iri goma*)
 2 tsp + more for garnishing

White radish sprouts (*kaiware daikon*)
 1 packet, washed and halved

Usukuchi soy sauce 1/4 tsp

Shredded nori seaweed (*kizaminori*)
 for garnishing

This flavourful dish does not require cooking at all. If
you have steamed rice ready, you can start your meal in
5 minutes. To ensure freshness and good taste, choose
cod roe of good quality and prepare everything just
before serving.

1. Insert the tip of a knife into cod roe sac to slit it open.
 Using a spoon or the dull side of the knife, carefully scrape
 out the cod roe into a clean dry bowl.

2. Mix 2 tsp olive oil and lemon juice into the roe.

3. Wash preserved seaweed (wakame) and soak in water for
 5 minutes. Cut into 3-cm (1¼-in) strips.

4. Mix rice with sesame seeds and scoop into serving bowls.

5. Mix white radish sprouts, preserved seaweed (wakame),
 usukuchi soy sauce and remaining olive oil, then arrange
 onto rice. Top with spicy cod roe. Garnish with shredded
 nori seaweed and remaining sesame seeds before serving.

Smoked Salmon Don
Sumokusamon Don

I learnt about this dish from a Japanese friend who used to stay in New Zealand. Initially sceptical about this recipe, I was amazed that it actually works! You can substitute salmon with ham if you like.

SERVES 2

Yellow onion 1, peeled and both ends trimmed
Fresh lemon juice 1 tsp
Salt a pinch
Steamed rice 400 g (14 oz), at room temperature
Toasted white sesame seeds (*iri goma*) 2 Tbsp
Smoked salmon 100 g (3¹/₂ oz)
Pickled capers 10
SAUCE
Japanese mayonnaise 2 Tbsp
Wasabi ¹/₈ tsp
Usukuchi soy sauce 1 Tbsp
Extra virgin olive oil 1 tsp
Fresh lemon juice ¹/₄–¹/₂ tsp

1. Mix all sauce ingredients together. Set aside.

2. Slice onion very thinly and parallel to the lines so that you get thin strips. Soak onion strips in water for 10 minutes. Drain and pat dry.

3. Mix lemon juice and salt, then stir into rice and scatter sesame seeds over.

4. Spread onion strips over rice, then arrange smoked salmon and pickled capers on top.

5. Serve with sauce at the side.

Whitebait Don
Shirasu Don

Shirasu, or cooked whitebait, is rich in calcium. Studies show that every 100 g (3$\frac{1}{2}$ oz) of this healthy fish contains 500 mg of calcium. Because of its tender flesh, it is often used for baby food. It also goes well with salad, pasta or omelette. If you wish to reduce the salt in *shirasu*, blanch it before use.

SERVES 2

Steamed rice 400 g (14 oz)

Shredded nori seaweed (*kizaminori*) 4 Tbsp

Japanese cucumber 1

Cooked whitebait (*shirasu*) 100 g (3$\frac{1}{2}$ oz)

Sesame oil 2 tsp

Fresh egg yolks for raw consumption 2

Fine bonito flakes (*katsuobushi*) 2 Tbsp

Sashimi soy sauce to taste

1. Scoop half a serving of rice in each serving bowl. Scatter shredded nori seaweed over and cover with remaining rice.

2. Quarter cucumber lengthwise and remove the seeds. Cut into 1-cm ($\frac{1}{2}$-in) lengths. Mix with whitebait and sesame oil. Arrange mixture over rice, leaving a well in the centre. Drop a raw egg yolk in the well. Repeat for the other serving.

3. Garnish with fine bonito flakes and serve with sashimi soy sauce. This is best eaten with all ingredients mixed together. Season to taste with sashimi soy sauce.

Note: To reduce the salt content of whitebait, bring a pot of water to a boil and blanch it briefly. Drain and leave to cool to room temperature before use.

Soy Sauce

It is not an exaggeration to say that you cannot cook Japanese food without soy sauce. An essential seasoning like miso, Japanese soy sauce is made from soy beans, wheat and salt.

Steamed soy beans are mixed with wheat and *koji*, a type of fungus made from rice, barley or soy beans. From this, soy sauce *koji* (*shoyu koji*) is produced. Salt water is mixed in, and then it goes through a long process of fermentation before completion. In this book, I use three varieties of soy sauce: koikuchi, usukuchi and sashimi soy sauce.

Koikuchi soy sauce is dark soy sauce, mainly used in the Kanto region.

Usukuchi soy sauce is lighter in colour and used when you do not want to make your food look dark. This type of soy sauce is often used in the Kansai region, and contains more salt than koikuchi soy sauce.

Sashimi soy sauce is slightly sweetened and used as a dipping sauce for raw fish. If you want to avoid sweetness, you can use koikuchi or usukuchi soy sauce.

Any type of soy sauce oxidises quickly once the bottle is opened, so it is better to use it up as soon as possible and keep it refrigerated to preserve its flavour. For those with dietary restrictions, low-sodium or gluten-free soy sauces are available.

Tofu Steak Don
Okonomiyaki Style Don

Okonomiyaki is a Japanese-style savoury pancake. For this dish, firm beancurd is used to reproduce the taste of *okonomiyaki*. Full of flavours from vegetables and sauces, this makes a very satisfying and hearty meal.

SERVES 2

Canola oil for frying
Steamed rice 400 g (14 oz)
Bonito flakes (*katsuobushi*) 8 Tbsp
Mirin 1/4 tsp
Koikuchi soy sauce 1/4 tsp
Beijing cabbage 140 g (5 oz), cut into 3-cm (1 1/4-in) squares
Tonkatsu sauce 1–2 tsp
Japanese mayonnaise for garnishing
Chopped spring onions (scallions) for garnishing
TOFU STEAK
Firm beancurd (*tau kwa*) 2
Koikuchi soy sauce 2 Tbsp
Sake 2 tsp
Mirin 2 tsp
Nori seaweed 4 sheets, each 7 x 7 cm (3 x 3 in)
Pizza cheese 6 Tbsp
Plain (all-purpose) flour 3 Tbsp
Water 4 Tbsp
Fine bonito flakes (*katsuobushi*) 8 Tbsp

1. Prepare tofu steak. Horizontally divide beancurd into 3 layers. Marinate in koikuchi soy sauce, sake and mirin for 15 minutes. Flip beancurd layers and marinate the other side for another 15 minutes.

2. On the bottom beancurd layer, place 1 sheet of nori seaweed and scatter pizza cheese over. Place the second beancurd layer on top and repeat the layering, then cover with the top beancurd layer.

3. Stir flour and water to combine. Apply mixture on all sides of stuffed beancurd. Cover all sides with bonito flakes, patting with your palm so that they stick well.

4. Heat oil in a non-stick pan. Fry beancurd until cooked on all sides. Remove from heat and set aside.

5. Scoop half a serving of rice into each serving bowl. Mix bonito flakes, mirin and koikuchi soy sauce. Spread mixture over the rice, then cover with remaining rice.

6. Heat oil in a pan, stir-fry cabbage until soft, then season with tonkatsu sauce.

7. Arrange cabbage over rice. Top with tofu steak.

8. Garnish with mayonnaise and spring onions before serving.

Squid and Cabbage Don
Shiokara Don

Ika no shiokara, or preserved squid, is commonly sold in jars and typically served with steamed rice. Like preserved anchovies, *shiokara* can also be used to add flavour and saltiness to a dish.

SERVES 2

Emperor mushrooms 150 g (5$^1/_3$ oz)

Unsalted butter 20 g ($^2/_3$ oz)

Garlic 2 cloves, peeled and sliced

Preserved squid (*ika no shiokara***)** 1$^1/_2$ Tbsp

Red chilli 1, diagonally sliced

Beijing cabbage 300 g (10$^1/_2$ oz), cut into 3-cm (1$^1/_4$-in) squares

Mirin 1 Tbsp

Ground black pepper to taste

Salt (optional) to taste

Steamed rice 400 g (14 oz)

1. Remove the joints of emperor mushrooms. Slice into 3-cm (1$^1/_4$-in) strips, each 0.5 cm ($^1/_4$ in) thick.

2. Melt butter in a pan. Fry garlic until fragrant, then add preserved squid, chilli and emperor mushrooms.

3. Add cabbage and stir-fry. Season with mirin and pepper. Add salt if desired.

4. Serve on rice and garnish with pepper.

Creamy Chicken Don
Tori no Cream Don

You might find the combination of *dashi* and cream strange, and I must say many Japanese feel the same way. But give this recipe a try and you will realise that dairy products and *dashi* create a wonderful marriage of flavours.

SERVES 2

Boneless chicken leg 200 g (7 oz), cut into 3-cm (1¼-in) cubes

Salt to taste

Ground white pepper to taste

Plain (all-purpose) flour 1 tsp + more for dusting

Canola oil 1 Tbsp

Yellow onion ½, peeled and thinly sliced

Sake 4 Tbsp

Potatoes 150 g, peeled and cubed

Carrot 100 g (3½ oz), peeled and cubed

Japanese stock (*dashi*) 400 ml (13½ fl oz)

Whipping cream 200–300 ml (6¾– 10 fl oz)

Usukuchi soy sauce 2–3 tsp

Steamed rice 400 g (14 oz)

Unsalted butter 1 tsp

English parsley or chopped spring onions (scallions) for garnishing

1. Season chicken cubes with salt and pepper for about 5 minutes. Dust with flour.

2. Heat oil in a pan. Cook chicken until it changes colour, then add onion and stir-fry briefly.

3. Add sake. Allow the alcohol to evaporate before adding potatoes, carrot and 350 ml (11¾ fl oz) stock. Gently stir until chicken and vegetables are cooked through. As you cook, add remaining stock if too dry.

4. Stir in whipping cream, then add usukuchi soy sauce. Season with salt and pepper.

5. Combine butter and 1 tsp flour. Stir into the pan to thicken the mixture.

6. Serve on rice and garnish with English parsley or chopped spring onions.

Spicy Minced Pork and Eggplant Miso Don
Nasu Niku Miso Don

This is inspired by the famous Sichuan dish *ma po dou fu* (spicy stir-fried tofu and minced meat). As this recipe is meant to suit Japanese taste buds, use more chilli bean paste if you prefer a spicier taste.

SERVES 2

Japanese eggplant (brinjal / aubergine) 200 g, cut into 4-cm (1³/₄-in) lengths
Chicken bones soup granules ¹/₂ Tbsp
Water 300 ml (10 fl oz / 1¹/₄ cups)
Hatcho miso ¹/₂ Tbsp
Sesame oil for stir-frying and seasoning
Minced pork 150 g (5¹/₃ oz)
Old ginger 1 tsp, peeled and minced
Garlic ¹/₂ tsp, peeled and minced
Chilli bean paste ¹/₂ Tbsp
Oyster sauce 1 Tbsp
Sake ¹/₂ Tbsp
Johakuto sugar ¹/₂ Tbsp
Potato starch 1 Tbsp + 3 Tbsp water
Steamed rice 400 g (14 oz)
Shredded Japanese leek for garnishing

1. Soak eggplant in salted water for 10 minutes. Drain and set aside.

2. Prepare stock mixture. Mix chicken bones soup granules, water and hatcho miso. Stir well and set aside.

3. Heat oil in a pan. Stir-fry minced pork over medium heat. Add ginger and garlic when meat browns. Stir-fry until fragrant. Add about 1 Tbsp oil and egg plant to the pan.

4. Add chilli bean paste. Stir-fry briefly, then add stock mixture. When eggplant has been cooked through, add oyster sauce, sake, and sugar. Simmer for 3 minutes.

5. Stir in potato starch mixture to thicken. Season with a dash of sesame oil.

6. Serve on rice and garnish with shredded leek.

Classic and Traditional

Teriyaki Chicken Don
Tori no Teriyaki Don

Teriyaki means "grilled and glazed" or "pan-fried and glazed". Teriyaki sauce is very versatile. It can go with almost all kinds of meat and fish. One of the most popular dishes, this sweet and savoury combination is an all-time favourite.

SERVES 2

Boneless chicken leg 300 g (10½ oz)
Salt to taste
Ground black pepper to taste
Canola oil for pan-frying
Steamed rice 400 g (14 oz)
Sliced Japanese cucumber for garnishing
Toasted white sesame seeds (*iri goma*) for garnishing
Mixed chilli powder (*shichimi* / *nanami togarashi*) for seasoning
Japanese mayonnaise for seasoning
TERIYAKI SAUCE
Koikuchi soy sauce 40 ml (1²/₅ fl oz)
Johakuto sugar 15–20 g (½–²/₃ oz)
Sake 10 ml (⅓ fl oz)
Mirin 4 Tbsp

1. Heat all ingredients for teriyaki sauce in a pan. Simmer until the mixture reduces by half. Set aside.

2. Remove yellow fat from chicken meat. Sprinkle over salt and pepper.

3. Heat oil in a pan. Pan-fry chicken over medium heat until both sides have browned.

4. Cover with a lid and cook chicken over low heat. When chicken is cooked through, remove from the pan.

5. Clean the pan with paper towels and pour in teriyaki sauce. Place chicken in the sauce and heat until the meat is glazed and the sauce thickens.

6. Slice chicken into strips and place on rice. Pour sauce over.

7. Garnish with cucumber and toasted white sesame seeds.

8. Serve with mixed chilli powder and Japanese mayonnaise.

Braised Vegetable Don
Kanbutsu Don

Dried radish (*kiriboshi daikon*) and hijiki seaweed are my must-have items in the kitchen at all times. They are rich in minerals such as calcium, magnesium, vitamin C and dietary fibres. This is a braised dish that keeps well in the freezer, so you can cook big quantities at one go. It is also great as a side dish for *bento* lunchboxes.

SERVES 2

Dried radish (*kiriboshi daikon*) 25 g
   ($^4/_5$ oz)

Hijiki seaweed 8 g ($^1/_5$ oz)

Sesame oil 2 Tbsp

Carrot 25 g ($^4/_5$ oz), peeled and cut into
   0.5-cm ($^1/_4$-in) strips

Deep-fried bean curd puff (*aburaage*)
   $^1/_2$, blanched and cut into 0.5-cm
   ($^1/_4$-in) strips

Japanese stock (*dashi*) 300 ml
   (10 fl oz / $1^1/_4$ cups)

Johakuto sugar 1 Tbsp

Sake 1 Tbsp

Usukuchi soy sauce $1^1/_2$–2 Tbsp

Eggs 2

Steamed rice 400 g (14 oz)

1. Soak dried radish in water for about 10 minutes until it softens. Do the same for hijiki seaweed.

2. Heat oil in a pot over medium heat. Stir-fry dried radish and hijiki seaweed for 3 minutes.

3. Add carrot and bean curd puff. Stir-fry for 2 minutes.

4. Stir in stock, sugar, sake and usukuchi soy sauce. Braise vegetables by turning to low heat and simmering until the liquid almost evaporates. Remove from heat.

5. Add half of the braised vegetables in a small pan. Cover with a lid and bring to a boil over medium heat. Crack an egg into a bowl. Make a well in the centre of the braised vegetables and gently pour egg into it. Turn heat to medium-low and cook until the egg white is firm but the yolk is still runny. Gently place on top of rice so that the egg yolk is not broken. Repeat for the other serving.

6. Mix all ingredients together, using the yolk as a sauce.

Note: If preparing this for a lunchbox (*bento*), make sure that the eggs are fully cooked.

Ginger Pork Don
Buta No Shougayaki Don

This is a typical Japanese home-style dish. Grated ginger not only tenderises the meat and removes any pungent smell from pork, it also gives a wonderful taste to the meat. There are no words to describe just how much I love this dish.

SERVES 2

Ginger juice 1 Tbsp

Sake 2 Tbsp

Pork loin or shoulder 300 g (10^1/$_2$ oz), cut into 4 mm (^{1}/$_4$ in) thick slices

Yellow onion 1, peeled and both ends trimmed

Vegetable oil for frying

Steamed rice 400 g (14 oz)

Shredded cabbage for garnishing

Sliced Japanese cucumber for garnishing

SAUCE

Old ginger 30 g (1 oz), grated

Koikuchi soy sauce 65 ml (2^1/$_5$ fl oz)

Mirin 45 ml (1^1/$_2$ fl oz)

Johakuto Sugar 1^1/$_2$ Tbsp

1. Mix ginger juice and sake. Marinate pork slices in the mixture for 5 minutes.

2. Mix all sauce ingredients together. Set aside.

3. Slice onion very thinly and parallel to the lines so that you get thin strips.

4. Heat oil in a pan over medium heat. Stir-fry onion until half translucent. Remove from heat and set aside.

5. Briefly marinate pork in the sauce. Heat oil in a pan and cook both sides of the pork for 1 minute. Remove from heat and set aside.

6. Wipe the pan with paper towels. Pour in sauce and bring to a boil. Return pork and onion to the pan. When pork slices are coated with sauce, remove from heat.

7. Serve pork and onion on rice and drizzle sauce over. Garnish with shredded cabbage and cucumber.

Miso Short Neck Clam Don
Fukagawa Don

Asari, or short neck clams, are flavourful and go very well with rice. Deliciously savoury, this is one of Tokyo's specialities.

SERVES 2

Water 180 ml (6 fl oz / ³/₄ cup)

Short neck clams (*asari*) 24

Johakuto sugar 1 tsp

Mirin 2 tsp

Shinshu miso 2 tsp

Japanese leek 1¹/₂ stalks, diagonally sliced

Steamed rice 400 g (14 oz)

Chopped spring onions (scallions) for garnishing

Shredded old ginger for garnishing

1. Boil water in a pot. Cook clams with a lid on until the shells open. Drain and set clams aside. Reserve clam stock.

2. Measure out 140 ml (4³/₄ fl oz) of clam stock. Add water if there isn't enough liquid. Bring to a boil in a pot.

3. Lower heat. Add sugar and mirin. Place shinshu miso onto a strainer or sieve and lower into pot. Using the back of a spoon or a spatula, Strain miso into the mixture. Add leek and simmer.

4. When leek softens, add clams and simmer for 2 minutes.

5. Serve on rice, with spring onions and shredded old ginger by the side for garnishing.

Note: If using fresh clams, soak in salted water for about 3 hours to let them expel sand and dirt.

Grilled Miso Cod Don
Tara No Miso Yaki Don

This is a restaurant-style dish that you can easily prepare at home. You can use store-bought miso-marinated cod, but the marinating ingredients are so simple that you can do it by yourself. Snapper, salmon and sierra are also suitable for this recipe. If you do not have a grill, use a non-stick frying pan lined with greased aluminum foil.

SERVES 2

Cod fish fillets 2, each about 130 g (4^2/$_3$ oz)

Sea salt ^{1}/$_2$ tsp

Canola oil for greasing

Celery 1 stalk

Sweet pickled ginger (*gari*) 1 Tbsp, sliced

Steamed rice 400 g (14 oz)

MISO MARINADE

Shinshu miso 110 g (4 oz)

Mirin 2 Tbsp

Johakuto sugar 1^1/$_2$ Tbsp

1. Marinate cod fillets with sea salt for 20 minutes. Rinse away salt and pat dry with paper towels.

2. Mix all ingredients for miso marinade. Place fish fillets in a re-sealable bag and pour in marinade. Coat fillets evenly and leave to marinate in the refrigerator for more than 8 hours.

3. Cover a fish grill with aluminum foil and grease it. Place fish onto the greased foil and grill over high heat. If you do not have a grill, line a non-stick frying pan lined with greased aluminum foil, place fillets onto the foil and grill over high heat. Grill each side for 4 minutes.

4. Meanwhile, de-string celery and slice thinly. Mix with pickled ginger by squeezing with your hand. Set aside.

5. Serve grilled cod on rice and garnish with celery and pickled ginger.

Beef Don
Gyu Don

SERVES 2

Yellow onion 1, peeled and both ends trimmed

Japanese stock (*dashi*) 130 ml (4²/₅ fl oz)

Koikuchi soy sauce 45 ml (1¹/₂ fl oz)

Mirin 75 ml (2¹/₃ fl oz)

Beef 180 g (6¹/₃ oz), thinly sliced

Johakuto sugar (optional) 1 Tbsp

Steamed rice 400 g (14 oz)

Fresh eggs for raw consumption (optional) 2

Red pickled ginger (*beni shoga*) for garnishing

Popularly known as "beef bowl" outside Japan, the key to this great-tasting meal is to use very thinly sliced beef with some fat. Serve with fresh raw eggs for a richer taste.

1. Halve onion along it's lines. Place both halves with cut side facing down. Slice each half into 0.5-cm (¹/₄-in) strips, perpendicular to the onion grains.

2. In a pot, bring stock, koikuchi soy sauce and mirin to a boil. Add onion. Cook until tender and translucent.

3. Add beef. Stir well with chopsticks. Remove from heat before beef is completely cooked. If you prefer a sweeter taste, add sugar.

4. Serve on rice with raw eggs if desired. Garnish with red pickled ginger.

Japonica Rice

In Japan, rice is harvested in autumn (except in Okinawa). Every year, I am excited during the season when rice is harvested. This is when I feel most grateful for the blessings of nature. New rice shines like pearls and is very sweet.

Japonica or Japanese rice are short-grained, and contains more starch than long-grain rice. If not washed thoroughly, the starch in the rice grains will produce an unpleasant smell when cooked, and the rice will become too sticky. It is therefore important to rinse the rice grains properly before cooking (see page 132).

It is difficult to tell whether rice is fresh just by looking at it, so it is best to check the packaging date. Unless it is new rice season, it is best to buy brown rice, get it polished, and use it up as soon as possible. Otherwise, choose white rice with the latest expiration date.

Rice goes bad very quickly during hot weather, so it is better to keep rice refrigerated if possible. If storing at room temperature, keep rice in a sealed container and in a cool shady area away from direct sunlight.

Beef and Burdock Yanagawa-style Don
Gyu Yanagawa Don

Yanagawa was one of the Japanese domains during the historical Edo period. In the original recipe, loach is used instead of beef. This is also one of Tokyo's specialities, and my husband's favourite way of replenishing energy when he's feeling tired.

SERVES 2

Burdock (*gobo*) 70 g (2¹/₂ oz), peeled

Beef, short rib or other parts with fat 80 g (2⁴/₅ oz), thinly sliced into 3-cm (1¹/₄-in) lengths

Eggs 4

Steamed rice 400 g (14 oz)

Chopped spring onions (scallions) for garnishing

SEASONING

Japanese stock (*dashi*) 200 g (7 oz)

Johakuto sugar 2 Tbsp

Koikuchi soy sauce 2¹/₂–3 Tbsp

Sake 2 tsp

Mirin 2 tsp

1. Using a peeler, julienne burdock into 5-cm (2-in) strips. Soak in water for 10 minutes. Drain and pat dry with paper towels. Set aside.

2. Heat seasoning ingredients in a pot and bring to a boil. Lower to medium heat. Cook burdock until tender, then add beef. Stir to cook until beef has browned. Remove from heat.

3. Place half of the beef mixture in a small skillet or *donburi* pot. Cover with a lid and bring to a boil. Stir in 2 eggs. Cover with a lid until eggs are cooked to desired level of doneness. Remove from heat and place on rice. Repeat for the other serving.

4. Garnish with spring onions and serve.

Miso Mackerel Don
Saba no Miso ni Don

One of the most popular Japanese home-style dishes,
this is a pleasant dish that tastes as good as it looks.
The unique taste of mackerel is enhanced by miso,
and the delicious blend of all the ingredients will make
anyone ask for more.

SERVES 2

Mackerel fillets 2, about 110 g
  (4 oz) each
Salt a sprinkle
Water 250 ml (8 fl oz / 1 cup)
Sake 100 ml (3^1/₃ fl oz)
Johakuto sugar ^{1}/₂ Tbsp
Koikuchi soy sauce ^{1}/₂ Tbsp
Old ginger slices 3
Shinshu miso 1^1/₂–2 Tbsp
Saikyo miso 1^1/₂–2 Tbsp
Grain vinegar (_kokumotsu su_) ^{1}/₂ tsp
Mirin ^{1}/₂ Tbsp
Potato starch 1 tsp + 1 Tbsp water
Steamed rice 400 g (14 oz)
Japanese leek 1 stalk, white part only,
  shredded
Old ginger 2.5-cm (1-in) knob, grated
Chopped spring onions (scallions) for
  garnishing

1. Marinate mackerel fillets with a sprinkle of salt for 20 minutes.
   Blanch fillets briefly and chill in iced water. Remove dark red
   flesh and pat dry with paper towels.

2. Place mackerel fillets in a pot. Add water and sake. Cover with
   a drop lid and cook over high heat. When boiling, reduce to
   medium heat and remove scum. Add sugar. Simmer with the
   drop lid on.

3. When the liquid has reduced by a quarter, add koikuchi
   soy sauce and continue to simmer with the drop lid on for
   5 minutes.

4. Remove the drop lid and set it aside. There is no need for the
   drop lid from this point onwards. Add ginger slices, shinshu
   and saikyo miso. Simmer for another 5 minutes.

5. When the gravy becomes slightly thick, add grain vinegar,
   reduce to low heat until it simmers.

6. Add mirin and leave to simmer. Stir in potato starch mixture
   to thicken. Remove from heat and place mackerel fillets onto
   rice. Pour gravy over mackerel fillets.

7. Serve with shredded leek, ginger and spring onions.

Note: The drop lid is a common Japanese cooking equipment, which
is a wooden lid especially useful for simmering dishes. It ensures food
is evenly cooked and prevents the ingredients from moving around
so that they retain their shape. If you don't have a drop lid, make one
using an aluminum sheet. Cut it such that it can fit inside your pot,
and make a small hole in the centre for ventilation.

Chicken and Egg Don
Oyako Don

Oya means "parent" and *ko* means "child". A typical *oyakodon* has chicken and eggs, which explains why it is named as such. Another reason for this name is its popularity with people of all ages, as both the young and old enjoy this dish a lot.

SERVES 2

Boneless chicken leg with skin 200–250 g (7–9 oz)

Yellow onion 1, peeled and both ends trimmed

Eggs 4, beaten

Steamed rice 400 g (14 oz)

Japanese parsley (*mitsuba*) or spring onions (scallions) for garnishing

SAUCE

Mirin 25 ml ($^4/_5$ fl oz)

Japanese stock (*dashi*) 225 ml ($7^2/_3$ fl oz)

Koikuchi soy sauce 70 ml ($2^1/_3$ fl oz)

Johakuto sugar about 1 Tbsp

1. Remove excess yellow fat from the chicken and cut into bite-size pieces.

2. Slice onion very thinly and parallel to the lines so that you get thin strips.

3. Prepare sauce. Pour mirin into a pot and bring to a boil. Add stock, koikuchi soy sauce and sugar. Simmer until the sugar dissolves.

4. Divide all ingredients into two portions to cook each serving individually.

5. Pour sauce into a small pan. Add chicken and cook for a few minutes with onion. Stir in beaten eggs and cover with a lid. After half a minute, uncover pan and cook until eggs are half done. Remove from heat and place onto rice. Repeat for the other serving.

6. Garnish with Japanese parsley or spring onions. Serve immediately.

Breaded Pork Cutlet and Egg Don
Katsu Don

This is a typical *donburi* dish that is popular because deep-fried breaded pork tastes so good with eggs. If you like half-cooked eggs like me, use fresh eggs that are good enough for raw consumption.

SERVES 2

Yellow onion $1/2$, peeled and thinly sliced

Eggs 4, beaten

Steamed rice 400 g (14 oz)

Japanese parsley (*mitsuba*) or spring onions (scallions) for garnishing

DEEP-FRIED PORK CUTLET (TONKATSU)

Pork loin or shoulder 2 cuts, about 130 g ($4^2/3$ oz) each

Salt to taste

Ground white pepper to taste

Plain (all-purpose) flour for dusting

Egg 1, beaten, for coating

Breadcrumbs for coating

Vegetable oil for deep frying

SAUCE

Mirin 2 Tbsp

Japanese stock (*dashi*) 200 ml ($6^3/4$ fl oz)

Koikuchi soy sauce 3 Tbsp

Johakuto sugar $1/2$ Tbsp

1. Prepare deep-fried pork. Tenderise pork with a mallet. Sprinkle salt and pepper on both sides.

2. Lightly dust with flour, then dip in egg, followed by breadcrumbs.

3. Heat oil to 160°C (325°F) in a heavy pot. Deep-fry pork until it browns. Flip pork over and increase heat to 180°C (350°F). Deep-fry until crispy.

4. Remove from heat and drain off oil on a wire rack. Leave to cool.

5. Meanwhile, prepare sauce. Pour mirin into a pot and bring to a boil. Add stock, koikuchi soy sauce and sugar. Simmer until the sugar dissolves.

6. Divide all ingredients into two portions to cook each serving individually.

7. Heat sauce and onion in a small skillet and cook for a few minutes. Slice pork cutlet into 1.5-cm ($3/4$-in) strips and add to the skillet. Pour eggs over cutlet and cover with a lid. After half a minute, uncover pan and cook until eggs are half done. Remove from heat and place onto rice. Repeat for the other serving.

8. Garnish with Japanese parsley or spring onions. Serve immediately.

Note: If preparing this for a lunchbox (*bento*), make sure that the eggs are fully cooked.

Miso Pork Cutlet Don
Miso Katsu Don

SERVES 2

Shredded Beijing cabbage for garnishing

Steamed rice 400 g (14 oz)

Toasted white sesame seeds (*iri goma*) for garnishing

DEEP-FRIED PORK CUTLET (TONKATSU)

See page 75.

MISO SAUCE

Hatcho miso 2¹/₂–3 Tbsp

Johakuto sugar 1 Tbsp

Japanese stock (*dashi*) 35 ml (1¹/₅ fl oz)

Mirin 1 Tbsp

Koikuchi soy sauce ¹/₂ Tbsp

Hatcho miso is used for the sauce in this dish. It is dark brown and more salty than other types of miso. A Nagoya speciality, *hatcho* miso is traditionally used as a dipping sauce for *oden*, which are stewed winter dishes such as radish, fish cakes and *konnyaku* (yam cake). This versatile sauce goes well with crunchy pork cutlet and steaming rice, making this a deliciously savoury meal.

1. Mix all ingredients for miso sauce in a small pan. Stir well and simmer until it thickens slightly. Remove from heat.

2. Arrange shredded cabbage over rice. Slice each pork cutlet into 2.5-cm (1-in) strips and place on top of cabbage.

3. Garnish with toasted sesame seeds and serve with miso sauce.

Wasabi

This well known condiment is most famous in the form of a green paste served alongside sashimi (raw seafood) and sushi. However, wasabi can be served with many other kinds of food, as its unique, pungent taste complements certain food very well. However, this unique taste will be lost if subject to too much heat.

Wasabi is available in three forms: fresh, powdered or paste. Fresh wasabi is obtained by grating the root of the wasabi plant in circular motions. Powdered wasabi is derived from horseradish, and does not contain the authentic colour or taste of the wasabi plant. This is a cheaper alternative and has to be mixed with water into a paste before consumption. Wasabi paste comes in a tube and may be made from the wasabi plant or horseradish, and it usually contains green colouring.

Regardless of the type of wasabi, it must be stored in the refrigerator, except wasabi powder, which can be kept at room temperature until mixed with water into a paste.

Tricolor Don
Sansyoku Don

I remember this as one of my favourite *bento* meals when I was young. My mother used to prepare this whenever she did not have time to cook many items on busy mornings. It is a delightfully fun mix of sweet and savoury flavours that can be whipped up quickly and easily.

SERVES 2

Carrot 3-cm (1¼-in) length, peeled and thinly sliced

French beans 4, strings removed and diagonally sliced

Steamed rice 400 g (14 oz)

Shredded nori seaweed (*kizaminori*) for garnishing

MINCED CHICKEN SPRINKLES

Sake 4 Tbsp

Koikuchi soy sauce 3 Tbsp

Johakuto sugar 2 Tbsp

Water 4 Tbsp

Minced chicken 200 g (7 oz)

SWEET SCRAMBLED EGGS

Eggs 2

Egg yolk 1

Canola oil 1 tsp

Johakuto sugar ½–1 Tbsp

Salt a pinch

1. Prepare minced chicken sprinkles. Mix sake, koikuchi soy sauce, sugar and water in a pan. Stir in minced chicken. Use 2 or more cooking chopsticks for easy stirring. When well mixed, place pan over medium heat and keep stirring until chicken is cooked. Simmer until the liquid has almost evaporated. Leave to cool to room temperature.

2. Mix all ingredients for sweet scrambled eggs in a pan. Stir well with 2 or more cooking chopsticks. When well mixed, place pan over medium-low heat and keep stirring until eggs are cooked and scrambled into fine bits. Remove from heat and keep stirring until it cools to room temperature. Set aside.

3. Using a cookie cutter, cut carrot into desired shapes. Boil water with a pinch of salt. Blanch carrot and French beans, then chill in iced water. Drain and set aside.

4. Lightly pat rice to flatten the surface. Arrange chicken sprinkles, scrambled eggs and vegetables over rice. Garnish with shredded nori seaweed and serve.

Note: You can prepare bigger portions of chicken sprinkles as they can be kept frozen for up to two weeks. They are great as salad sprinkles or when mixed with mashed hard-boiled eggs and mayonnaise.

Katsu Sauce Don
Sosu Katsu Don

I was told by one of my foodie friends that this recipe must be included, as it is a speciality of the Fukui, Nagano and Yamanashi prefectures. This also happens to be one of my favourites, and I like it with lots of cabbage.

SERVES 2

Shredded Beijing cabbage for garnishing

Young mustard greens (*wasabi-na*) for garnishing

Steamed rice 400 g (14 oz)

Chopped spring onions (scallions) for garnishing

Japanese mustard (*karashi*) to taste

SAUCE

Tonkatsu or chuno sauce 80 ml (2¹/₂ fl oz / ¹/₃ cup)

Usutah sauce or Japanese style Worchester sauce 1 Tbsp

Dashi 1 Tbsp

Johakuto sugar 1¹/₂ Tbsp

Koikuchi soy sauce 1 tsp

DEEP-FRIED PORK CUTLET (TONKATSU)

See page 75.

1. Mix all sauce ingredients and stir well until sugar dissolves.

2. While pork cutlets are still hot, dip into the sauce and coat evenly. Cut into 2.5-cm (1-in) strips.

3. Arrange shredded cabbage and mustard greens over rice. Place pork cutlets on top.

4. Pour sauce over the pork cutlets. Garnish with spring onions and serve with Japanese mustard.

Potato Croquette Don
Poteto Korokke Don

This is a Western-inspired dish that is popular throughout Japan. Every family has their own recipe and here is my mother's. Substitute beef with other meats or add herbs and spices to make your own version of this dish.

SERVES 2

Vegetable oil for deep-frying

Shredded Beijing cabbage for garnishing

Steamed rice 400 g (14 oz)

Mayonnaise to taste

Tonkatsu sauce to taste

POTATO CROQUETTES

Potatoes 200 g (7 oz), washed, peeled and quartered

Vegetable oil or butter for stir-frying

Yellow onion 1/4, peeled and finely chopped

Minced beef 60 g (2 oz)

Unsalted butter 1 tsp

Whipping cream 2 tsp

Salt to taste

Ground black pepper to taste

Plain (all-purpose) flour for coating

Egg 1, beaten, for coating

Breadcrumbs for coating

1. Prepare potato croquettes. Boil potatoes in water until soft. Drain and mash.

2. Heat oil or butter in a pan. Stir-fry onion until half translucent. Add beef and stir-fry until cooked. Mix in mashed potatoes, then turn off heat. Add butter and whipping cream while hot. Season with salt and pepper.

3. Shape 2 patties with the mixture. Coat patties with flour, followed by egg, then breadcrumbs.

4. Heat oil to 175°C (347°F). Deep-fry patties until golden brown and crispy.

5. Arrange shredded cabbage over rice. Top with potato croquettes.

6. Serve with mayonnaise and tonkatsu sauce.

Grilled Eel and Egg Don
Unatama Don

Una or *unagi* means "eel", and *tama* or *tamago* means "egg". In Japan, there is a day during the hottest time in summer called *doyou no ushi no hi*, when many will consume *unagi*, which is believed to be able to counter summer fatigue.

SERVES 2

Grilled seasoned eel (*unagi kabayaki*) 200 g (7 oz), cut into bite-size pieces
Eggs 4
Steamed rice 400 g (14 oz)
Japanese parsley (*mitsuba*) for garnishing
Japanese pepper spice (*sansyo*) to taste
SAUCE
Koikuchi soy sauce 40 ml (1²/₅ fl oz)
Mirin 20 ml (²/₃ fl oz)
Johakuto sugar 1 Tbsp
Water 150 ml (5 fl oz)

1. Bring all ingredients for the sauce to a boil. Simmer for 3 minutes.

2. Pour half of the sauce in a small pan. Bring to a boil. Add half of the eel. In a bowl, lightly beat beat 2 eggs. Pour into the pan and lower heat. Cover with a lid until eggs are cooked to desired level of doneness. Remove from heat and place on rice. Repeat for the other serving.

3. Garnish with Japanese parsley and serve with Japanese pepper spice.

Omelette and Ketchup Don
Omurice Don

Omurice is a typical *Yoshoku* dish, a type of European-inspired Japanese cuisine. It usually takes the form of half a rugby ball, with ketchup-flavoured chicken rice wrapped in an omelette. Turning this into a *donburi* requires some adaptation, which actually makes it much easier to reproduce the same flavours. For a *donburi*, you simply need to make a soft flat omelette to place on top of the chicken rice. There is no need to ensure the omelette is in that perfect half-rugby shape.

SERVES 2

CHICKEN RICE
Unsalted butter ^{2}/$_3$ Tbsp
Canola oil ^{1}/$_2$ Tbsp
Yellow onion ^{1}/$_2$, peeled and chopped
Boneless chicken leg 150 g (5^1/$_3$ oz), cubed
Steamed rice 250 g (9 oz)
Frozen mixed vegetables 100 g (3^1/$_2$ oz)
Tomato ketchup 3 Tbsp
Chicken bones soup granules 1 tsp
Ground white pepper to taste
Sea salt to taste
OMELETTE
Eggs 4
Whipping cream 2 tsp
Ground white pepper to taste
Salt a pinch
Unsalted butter 1 Tbsp
Tomato ketchup for garnishing
Chopped English parsley for garnishing

1. Prepare chicken rice. Heat unsalted butter and oil in a pan. Stir-fry onion over medium-high heat until half translucent.

2. Add chicken and cook until done. Add rice and frozen mixed vegetables. Stir-fry until vegetables are completely heated.

3. Season with tomato ketchup, chicken bones soup granules, pepper and salt. Scoop into serving bowls.

4. Prepare omelette. Stir eggs with whipping cream, pepper and salt.

5. Heat half of the butter in a small pan. Pour in half of the egg mixture. While eggs are cooking, scratch the surface with chopsticks to fluff up the omelette. When omelette is soft and fluffy, place on top of chicken rice. Repeat to make another omelette.

6. Garnish with tomato ketchup and parsley. Serve immediately.

Special and Creative

Grilled Salted Rice Malt Chicken Don
Shiokoji Dori Don

Koji is rice malt that is used for making sake or miso. In recent years, it became popular to combine it with salt as a marinating ingredient for fish, meat and vegetables, hence the term *shiokoji* (*shio* means "salt"). *Shiokoji* can be easily made from *kome koji* (dry rice malt). Both of these are available in supermarkets, so you can either prepare home-made *shiokoji* or use store-bought ones. *Shiokoji* can also be used as a meat tenderiser and a substitute for salt, which means healthier meals as you can reduce the salt content during food preparation.

SERVES 2

Boneless chicken leg 300 g (10¹/₂ oz)

Salted rice malt (*shiokoji*) 5 tsp

Sesame oil 2¹/₂ Tbsp

Shiitake mushrooms 4

Canola oil for greasing

Japanese leek 20-cm (8-in) length, cut into 6 pieces

Koikuchi soy sauce 2 tsp

Steamed rice 400 g (14 oz)

Cucumber for garnishing

Mixed chilli powder (*shichimi / nanami togarashi*) for seasoning

SALTED RICE MALT (*SHIOKOJI*)

Dry rice malt (*kome kouji*) 200 g (7 oz)

Sea salt 55 g (2 oz)

Water about 250 ml (8 fl oz / 1 cup)

SHIOKOJI SAUCE

Salted rice malt (*shiokoji*) 2 Tbsp

Sesame oil 2 Tbsp

1. Prepare salted rice malt a week in advance. Break up dry rice malt if using the dry, solid type. Mix in salt by hand. Add water and stir well. Store in a sterilised jar and cover with cling film. Leave to ferment at room temperature for 1 week, stirring well once a day. Salted rice malt is ready for use when it turns fragrant and sweet. It can keep well in the refrigerator for up to 3 months.

2. Place chicken in a resealable bag. Pour in salted rice malt and sesame oil. Seal and gently squeeze to coat chicken evenly. Leave to marinate in the refrigerator overnight.

3. Wipe mushrooms with damp paper towels and remove stems.

4. Oil grill over high heat. If you do not have a grill, line a non-stick frying pan lined with greased aluminum foil. Lower to medium heat and grill chicken, leek and mushrooms until they brown. Season with koikuchi soy sauce.

5. Cut chicken into 1.5-cm (³/₄-in) strips. Place on rice with mushrooms and leek.

6. Garnish with cucumber and season with mixed chilli powder. Mix ingredients for *shiokoji* sauce to serve as a dip.

Beef Tendon and Radish Don
Gyu Suji Daikon Don

SERVES 2

Water 300 ml (10 fl oz / 1¼ cups)

Sake 50 ml (1⅔ fl oz) + 1 Tbsp

Beef tendon (*gyu suji*) 250 g (9 oz), cut into 3-cm (1¼-in) strips

Radish (*daikon*) 250 g (9 oz), peeled and cut into 3-cm (1¼-in) chunks

Steamed rice 400 g (14 oz)

Shredded Japanese leek 1 stalk, white part only, for garnishing

Japanese mustard (*karashi*) to taste

Mixed chilli powder (*shichimi / nanami togarashi*) to taste

SEASONING

Mirin 1 Tbsp

Johakuto sugar 1½ Tbsp

Koikuchi soy sauce 2½ Tbsp

Sake 1 Tbsp

Old ginger slices 2

Garlic 2 cloves, peeled and crushed

This is old-fashion Japanese pub food. Try this melt-in-your-mouth simmered beef tendon with fragrant steamed rice. You will love it.

1. Pour water and sake into a pressure cooker. Add beef, then close lid and lock it. Turn to maximum heat. When pressure has built up, lower heat and cook for 25 minutes. Turn off heat and unlock lid when it has cooled.

2. While cooking beef tendon, cook radish in another pot. Pour just enough water to immerse the radish. Simmer until soft. Drain and add radish into the pressure cooker. Mix in seasoning.

3. Close lid and lock pressure cooker. Turn to maximum heat. When pressure has built up, lower heat and cook for 5 minutes. When pressure cooker has cooled, open lid. Simmer until radish browns.

4. Scoop beef and radish onto rice. Top with shredded leek. Serve with Japanese mustard and mixed chilli powder.

Pork Belly Don
Buta Kakuni Don

This satisfying rice bowl is made with simmered pork belly, which tastes great with ramen too. Simmered pork can keep well in the freezer, so you can prepare a lot at a time. Cook eggs in gravy so that they absorb the flavours.

SERVES 2–3

Vegetable oil for pan-frying
Pork belly 450 g (1 lb)
Old ginger slices 4
Japanese leek 10-cm (4-in) length, green part only
Hardboiled eggs 2–3, peeled
Steamed rice 400 g (14 oz)
Blanched spinach or *chye sim* for garnishing
Shredded Japanese leek 1 stalk, white part only, for garnishing
Japanese mustard (*karashi*) to taste
GRAVY
Water 750 ml (24 fl oz / 3 cups)
Sake 6 Tbsp
Koikuchi soy sauce 4 Tbsp
Johakuto sugar 2–3 Tbsp
Mirin 1¹/₂ Tbsp
Grain vinegar (*kokumotsu su*) 2 tsp

1. Heat oil in a pan. Brown all sides of pork belly, then place in a pressure cooker.

2. Add ginger and leek. Fill with just enough water to immerse the pork. Close lid and lock it. Bring to a boil over high heat. When pressure has built up, lower to medium heat. Leave to simmer for 30–40 minutes before turning off the heat. When pressure cooker has cooled, open the lid to check if meat is tender enough. If not, continue to cook with the lid closed, checking every 10 minutes.

3. Drain pork and cut into 3-cm (1¹/₄-in) chunks.

4. Discard water, ginger and leek. Return pork to the pressure cooker. Clean the cooker first if necessary. Add hardboiled eggs and gravy ingredients into the cooker. Simmer for 30 minutes over low heat without closing the lid. Remove from heat and scoop onto rice.

5. Garnish with blanched vegetables and shredded leek. Serve with Japanese mustard.

Eight Treasure Don
Happosai Don

The *Happosai* or Eight Treasure Don is named thus because it traditionally contains eight main ingredients. Most probably influenced by Cantonese cuisine, this common dish in Japan can be prepared with any variety of meat or vegetables on hand.

SERVES 2

Squid 50 g (1²/₃ oz), cut into rings

Prawns 6, heads removed, shelled and deveined

Egg white from 1 egg

Potato starch 1 Tbsp

Salt a pinch

Ground white pepper a pinch

Canola oil for blanching and frying

Yellow onion ¼, peeled and thinly sliced

Chinese long cabbage 150 g (5¹/₃ oz), cut into 3-cm (1¹/₄-in) squares

Carrot 30 g (1 oz), thinly sliced

Snow peas 6 pods, ends trimmed and strings removed

Pork belly 50 g (1²/₃ oz), thinly sliced

Japanese leek ¼ stalk, thinly sliced

Chopped old ginger ¼ tsp

Minced garlic ¼ tsp

Hardboiled quail eggs 4, peeled

Potato starch 2 tsp + 2 Tbsp water

Sesame oil for flavouring

Steamed rice 400 g (14 oz)

SEASONING

Oyster sauce 4 tsp

Koikuchi soy sauce 1¹/₂ tsp

Johakuto sugar a pinch

Salt to taste

Chicken bones soup granules a pinch

Sake 3 Tbsp

Water 6 Tbsp

1. Coat squid and prawns with egg white, potato starch and a pinch of salt and pepper.

2. Boil water with 1 tsp canola oil in a pot. Blanch squid and prawns, then drain and plunge into ice water. Drain and pat dry with paper towels. Set aside.

3. Boil water with 1 tsp canola oil in a pot. Blanch onion, cabbage, carrot and snow peas. Drain. Set aside blanched vegetables, except snow peas. Plunge snow peas in iced water, then drain and slice to halve them before setting aside.

4. Meanwhile, combine all seasoning ingredients and set aside.

5. Heat 2 Tbsp canola oil in a wok or big pan over medium-high heat. Stir-fry pork briefly before adding leek, ginger and garlic. Fry until fragrant.

6. Increase to high heat. Add blanched seafood and vegetables, followed by quail eggs. Toss to mix and work fast.

7. Add seasoning ingredients to the wok or pan. Toss to mix well. Add potato starch mixture to thicken. Add more salt and pepper to taste if desired.

8. Drizzle sesame oil for flavour and serve on rice.

Foie Gras and Radish Don
Foa Gura Daikon Don

This is an appetising dish that combines the exquisite taste of foie gras and the mild flavour of radish. Being light and sweet, the radish absorbs and balances out the rich juices of foie gras, making this a wonderfully well blended dish.

SERVES 2

Radish (*daikon*) 250 g (9 oz), peeled and sliced into 0.5-cm ($^{1}/_{2}$-in) rounds

Water 400 ml (13$^{1}/_{2}$ fl oz)

Sake 20 ml ($^{2}/_{3}$ fl oz)

Chicken bones soup granules 1 Tbsp

Usukuchi soy sauce 1 Tbsp

Kelp (konbu) 1 sheet, about 4 x 4 cm (1$^{3}/_{4}$ x 1$^{3}/_{4}$ in)

Potato starch 1 tsp + 1 Tbsp water

Foie gras 200 g (7 oz), sliced

Salt to taste

Ground black pepper to taste

Plain (all-purpose) flour for dusting

Steamed rice 400 g (14 oz)

SAUCE

Sake 3 Tbsp

Balsamic vinegar 25 ml ($^{4}/_{5}$ fl oz)

Koikuchi soy sauce 35 ml (1$^{1}/_{5}$ fl oz)

Honey 4 tsp

Unsalted butter 1 Tbsp

1. Boil radish in a pot. It is not necessary to boil with water, but add just enough to cover radish if you prefer. Simmer over low heat until tender.

2. Drain and return radish to the pot. Add water, sake, chicken bones soup granules, usukuchi soy sauce and kelp. Bring to a boil, then simmer for about 20 minutes. Return to a boil again, then stir in potato starch mixture to thicken. Set aside.

3. Meanwhile, prepare sauce. Bring sake, balsamic vinegar, koikuchi soy sauce and honey to a boil. Lower heat and simmer until it thickens. Stir in butter. Set aside.

4. Season foie gras with salt and pepper. Dust with flour.

5. Pan-fry foie gras in a heated pan without oil, as the foie gras produces oil when heated. Do not cook for too long or it will shrink. Remove from heat when browned.

6. Arrange radish rounds over rice and spoon its gravy over. Top with foie gras.

7. Drizzle sauce over and serve.

Umeboshi

Umeboshi are preserved plums made from ripe *ume* fruits (Japanese plums), which are harvested around June. They are often cooked with fish, used as a filling in *onigiri* (Japanese rice balls), or cut into small bits for salad dressing.

There are various ways of preparing umeboshi, and the this is the traditional method used by my mother and other family members: Pack *ume* fruits with salt in a jar, then add a weight on top. The *ume* fruits should start to ooze liquid in a few days. Remove weight and add red shiso leaves. Return weight to the jar, cover and set aside. If red shiso leaves are not in season yet, keep *ume* fruits preserved in salt until shiso leaves are available. After the raining season (in Japan, this would be around end-July), take them out and dry them in the sun. Reserve the liquid and shiso leaves if you want more of the red colouring. You can choose to pack the dried *ume* fruits back in the jar together with the liquid and red shiso leaves, or store them as they are in their dried state. This traditional method yields very salty and sour preserved plums that can be kept for a long time in the refrigerator. It is said that these preserved plums taste better with age.

Today, there are new types of umeboshi available at supermarkets, for example, honey-flavoured or low-sodium umeboshi. For store-bought umeboshi, my preference is to choose those that are prepared using the simplest ingredients and processes, because umeboshi made using traditional methods are the tastiest and easiest to use for cooking. If you want to avoid taking too much salt, soak umeboshi in water before using.

Umeboshi contains citric acid, which is effective for countering fatigue. To feel refreshed in the morning, eat a small piece of umeboshi and you will be good to go.

Deep-fried Sweet and Sour Chicken Don
Tori no Nanban Zuke Don

The term *nanban* originally refers to Europeans, Dutch and Spanish in particular. Today, food with chilli are called *nanban*-style dishes, most probably because of their European-influenced flavours. The *nanban* sauce used here has a blend of sweet, sour and spicy flavours. It is versatile and can be used with many other ingredients such as white fish, salmon, pork, tofu or eggplant.

SERVES 2

Yellow onion 1, peeled and thinly sliced
Carrot 30 g (1 oz), peeled and julienned
Dried chilli 1, sliced
Boneless chicken leg 300 g (10¹/₂ oz), cut into bite-size pieces
Salt for seasoning
Ground black pepper for seasoning
Plain (all-purpose) flour for dusting
Canola oil for deep-frying
Steamed rice 400 g (14 oz)
Chopped spring onions (scallions) for garnishing
NANBAN SAUCE
Japanese stock (*dashi*) 150 ml (5 fl oz)
Johakuto sugar 3 Tbsp
Grain vinegar (*kokumotsu su*) 2 Tbsp
Koikuchi soy sauce 3 Tbsp

1. Soak onion slices in water for 10 minutes. Drain and set aside.

2. Combine all ingredients for *nanban* sauce in a pot. Bring to a boil over medium heat. Leave to cool to room temperature, then add carrot, onion and dried chilli. Set aside.

3. Season chicken with salt and pepper. Dust over with flour.

4. Heat oil to 170–180°C (338–350°F). Deep-fry chicken until the surface turns light brown. Remove from heat and leave on a wire rack for 3 minutes. Re-heat oil to 180°C (350°F). Return chicken to heated oil and deep-fry until golden brown.

5. While chicken is still hot, marinate in *nanban* sauce for at least 15 minutes.

6. Serve on rice and garnish with spring onions.

Crab and Salmon Roe Don
Hokkaido Don

SERVES 2

Snow peas 6 pods, ends trimmed and
  strings removed

Japanese stock (*dashi*) 150 ml (5 fl oz)

Usukuchi soy sauce 1 tsp

Mirin 20 ml (²/₃ fl oz)

Sake 2 tsp

Canned crab meat 150 g
  (5¹/₃ oz), drained

Boiled bamboo shoot a few slices,
  bottom part only

Steamed rice 400 g (14 oz), at room
  temperature

Salmon roe (*ikura*) 6 Tbsp

Shredded nori seaweed (*kizaminori*)
  for garnishing

OMELETTE RIBBONS

Egg 1

Salt a pinch

Johakuto sugar a pinch

Canola oil for frying

Infused with fragrant seafood flavours, this is a tasty
wholesome meal that is both sweet and savoury.

1. Prepare omelette ribbons. Stir egg, salt and sugar together.
   Heat oil in a non-stick pan over medium heat. Pour egg
   mixture and spread thinly over the pan. If using a small pan,
   split egg mixture to cook each serving separately. When the
   surface turns dry, turn over and cook for a few seconds.
   Remove from heat and shred very thinly into fine ribbons.
   Set aside.

2. Boil water in a small pan. Add a pinch of salt if desired, then
   blanch snow peas. Drain and chill in iced water. Set aside.

3. Pour stock, usukuchi soy sauce, mirin and sake into a pot.
   Add crab and bamboo shoot. Simmer over medium-low heat
   until the liquid is reduced by two-thirds. Leave to cool to
   room temperature.

4. Scatter crab meat over rice and top with salmon roe. Arrange
   bamboo shoot, snow peas and omelette ribbons as desired.

5. Garnish with shredded nori seaweed and serve.

Japanese Beef Steak Don
Bifuteki Don

Juicy beef and savoury onion soy sauce go absolutely well with fragrant steamed rice. If possible, use wagyu beef, which works best for this dish.

SERVES 2

Beef steak 2 slices, can be 100–200 g (3$^1/_2$–7 oz) each

Yellow onion $^1/_2$, peeled and sliced

Steamed rice 400 g (14 oz)

Vegetable oil 2 tsp

Small green peppers (*shishitogarashi*) for garnishing

SAUCE

Yellow onion $^1/_2$, peeled and grated

Koikuchi soy sauce 2 Tbsp

Mirin 2 Tbsp

Sake 1 Tbsp

Fuji apple 1, peeled and grated

Johakuto sugar 1 tsp

Unsalted butter 10 g ($^1/_3$ oz)

Grain vinegar (*kokumotsu su*) 1 tsp

Ground black pepper for seasoning

Salt (optional) for seasoning

1. Leave beef at room temperature for 2 hours.

2. Soak onion slices in water for 15 minutes. Drain and scatter over rice. Set aside.

3. Prepare sauce. Heat onion, koikuchi soy sauce, mirin, sake, grated apple and sugar in a pot. Bring to a boil. Lower heat and simmer for 10 minutes until the liquid is reduced by half. Add butter, grain vinegar and pepper. Season with salt if desired. Set aside.

4. Heat oil in a pan. Cook beef steaks for 2$^1/_2$ minutes on each side. Remove from heat and cover with aluminum foil for 10 minutes.

5. Return steaks to heated pan. Pour in half of the sauce and heat until it comes to a boil.

6. Remove from heat and slice steaks as desired. Serve on top of sliced onions and rice.

7. Garnish with small green peppers and serve with the sauce.

Note: While cooking beef, adjust heat according to desired level of doneness for the steaks.

Fried Scallops and Vegetable Don
Furai Don

This crunchy and savoury treat is a delight when served with three different sauces, one of which is shibazuke tartar sauce. Shibazuke is a pickled vegetable that is both sweet and sour. It makes a flavourful dip when paired with tartar sauce.

SERVES 2

Scallops 6, patted dry

Plain (all-purpose) flour for dusting

Egg 1, beaten, for coating

Breadcrumbs for coating

Hardboiled egg 2 quarters, shelled and halved

Asparagus spears 2, ends trimmed and cut into 4-cm (1¾-in) strips

Yellow onion ½, peeled and cut into 1-cm (½-in) slices

Vegetable oil for deep-frying

Steamed rice 400 g (14 oz)

Lettuce for garnishing

Cherry tomatoes for garnishing

Cucumber slices for garnishing

Tonkatsu sauce to taste

Japanese mustard (*karashi*) to taste

SHIBAZUKE TARTAR SAUCE

Yellow onion ¼, peeled and chopped

shibazuke 4 Tbsp, chopped

Hardboiled egg ½, chopped

Japanese mayonnaise 4 Tbsp

Ground white pepper for seasoning

1. Prepare shibazuke tartar sauce. Soak chopped onion in water for 15 minutes. Drain and mix with the rest of the ingredients for tartar sauce. Mix well and set aside.

2. Dust scallops with flour, then coat with egg, followed by breadcrumbs. Do the same for egg, asparagus and onion.

3. Heat oil to 170°C (338°F). Deep-fry battered ingredients until golden brown. Drain off oil on a wire rack before arranging over rice.

4. Garnish with lettuce, cherry tomatoes and cucumber. Serve with shibazuke tartar sauce, tonkatsu sauce and Japanese mustard.

Breaded Minced Pork and Cabbage Don
Menchi Katsu Don

Menchi is derived from the English word "minced". *Menchi katsu*, meaning deep-fried minced meat, can be made from pork or beef. Grated potato is used here to bind the minced meat together, resulting in juicier and more tender patties.

SERVES 2

Plain (all-purpose) flour for dusting

Egg 1, beaten, for coating

Panko breadcrumbs for coating

Canola oil for deep-frying

Shredded Beijing cabbage for garnishing

Steamed rice 400 g (14 oz)

Toasted white sesame seeds (*iri goma*) for garnishing

Japanese mustard to taste

BREADED PATTIES

Potato 60 g (2 oz), washed and peeled

Beijing cabbage 50 g (1²/₃ oz), coarsely chopped

Salt for seasoning

Ground black pepper for seasoning

Minced pork 150 g (5¹/₃ oz)

Ginger juice ¹/₂ tsp

Panko breadcrumbs 1 Tbsp

Oyster sauce 1 tsp

SAUCE

Tonkatsu sauce 2 Tbsp

Japanese mayonnaise 2 Tbsp

1. Prepare breaded patties. Grate potato and drain off excess water.

2. Mix cabbage with salt and let it sit for 10 minutes. Squeeze to remove excess moisture.

3. Mix all ingredients for breaded patties. Knead until everything is well combined and sticky. Shape into 2 patties.

4. Dust patties with flour, then dip in egg, followed by breadcrumbs. For a thicker breading, coat with egg and then breadcrumbs again.

5. Heat oil to 170°C (338°F). Deep-fry patties until golden brown. Leave on a wire rack to cool and drain off oil.

6. Meanwhile, mix sauce ingredients and set aside.

7. Scatter shredded cabbage over rice. Top with patties.

8. Drizzle sauce over and garnish with sesame seeds. Serve with Japanese mustard.

Obihiro Pork Don
Obihiro Buta Don

Obihiro is a city in Hokkaido, where this dish was made famous. Use a fish grill to cook the pork. Alternatively, it is recommended to use charcoal heat to impart a smoky taste that is excellent with soy sauce.

Pork belly or shoulder 350 g (12½ oz), thinly sliced

Salt for seasoning

Ground black pepper for seasoning

Canola oil for greasing

Steamed rice 400 g (14 oz)

Chopped spring onions (scallions) for garnishing

Shredded Japanese leek for garnishing

SAUCE

Johakuto sugar 3½ Tbsp

Water 2 tsp

Hot water 2 Tbsp

Koikuchi soy sauce 3 Tbsp

Sake 2 Tbsp

Mirin 2 Tbsp

1. Prepare sauce. Heat 2 Tbsp sugar and water over medium heat. When it turns a woody brown, turn off heat. Add hot water by letting it run down a wooden spatula. Stir well.

2. Stir in remaining sauce ingredients. Bring to a boil over medium-high heat. Remove from heat and set aside.

3. Lightly season one side of pork slices with salt and pepper. Heat and grease grill. If you do not have a grill, use a non-stick frying pan lined with greased aluminum foil. Cook both sides of pork slices.

4. Return sauce to the stove and bring to a boil. Add pork slices to glaze evenly. Season with pepper.

5. Arrange pork slices over rice. Garnish with spring onions and leek before serving.

Soy-marinated Tuna Sashimi Don
Maguro Zuke Don

If you have leftover tuna sashimi from the day before, it'll be great for this dish. The soy marinade will revive and enhance the taste of tuna sashimi. Do not use fatty *toro* tuna for this dish, as it will be too greasy.

SERVES 2

Hot steamed rice 400 g (14 oz)

Toasted white sesame seeds (*iri goma*) 2 Tbsp

Fresh raw tuna (*maguro* sashimi) 200–250 g (7–9 oz), thinly sliced

Shredded nori seaweed (*kizaminori*) for garnishing

Shiso leaves 2

Sweet pickled ginger (*gari*) for garnishing

Wasabi to taste

Sashimi soy sauce (optional) for seasoning

SUSHI VINEGAR

Grain vinegar (*kokumotsu su*) 1 Tbsp

Sea salt $^{1}/_{8}$ tsp

Johakuto sugar 2 tsp

SOY MARINADE

Koikuchi soy sauce 150 ml (5 fl oz)

Mirin 75 ml (2$^{1}/_{3}$ fl oz)

Sake 20 ml ($^{2}/_{3}$ fl oz)

1. Stir together all ingredients for sushi vinegar in a microwave-safe bowl. Heat in a microwave for 20 seconds, until salt and sugar have dissolved. Alternatively, heat over a stove. Pour over hot steamed rice. Scatter over sesame seeds and mix well. Leave to cool to room temperature.

2. Mix soy marinade ingredients in a shallow tray. Coat tuna slices evenly in marinade. Leave for 15 minutes.

3. Arrange marinated tuna slices over rice. Scatter over shredded nori seaweed.

4. Garnish with shiso leaves, pickled ginger and wasabi. Serve with sashimi soy sauce if desired.

Seaweed

Since Japan is surrounded by water, it is not surprising for the Japanese to use many ingredients from the sea, seaweed being one of them. Seaweed is generally low in calories. It is rich in calcium, iodine and fibre too. Here are the types of seaweed used in this book.

Kelp or konbu is essential to basic Japanese stock (*dashi*). Among the different kinds of kelp, the kinds used for Japanese stock are collectively known as *dashi* konbu, or named according to the production area, for example, Hidaka, Rishiri, Rausu konbu. These regions are in Hokkaido, which is famous for its konbu production. Konbu has blackish and dark green tones, with white powder on the surface. Never wash off this white powder as this is the source of umami, a pleasant savoury flavour. If you want to clean konbu, wipe it lightly with a well-squeezed damp kitchen towel. Konbu should be stored in a sealed container, away from heat or direct sunlight. For regions with tropical climate, I store konbu by cutting it into 4-cm (1³/₄-in) squares and refrigerate them in a sealed container. This is also convenient as you don't have to cut konbu each time you want to use it.

Wakame is softer than konbu. Its colour is also dark green but it is not as dark as konbu. Fresh wakame is available during spring in Japan. However, outside of Japan, you usually find salted wakame in the refrigerator section or dried wakame in a dried-food section at a supermarket. When using salted wakame, wash off salt and soak it in water until it becomes soft. If using the dried kind, simply soak it in water until it becomes soft, then cut according to how much you need. Wakame can be eaten raw and is good in salads. It is often used for miso soup together with tofu.

Nori is usually sold when dried and cooked. There is raw nori but it is rare. Sheets of nori are often used to wrap *onigiri* (Japanese rice balls) or sushi. Shredded nori (*kizaminori*) is usually used as a topping.

Hijiki is dried seaweed that comes in the form of black strings. Soak in water until it becomes soft before cooking.

Loco Moco Don
Rokomoko Don

Juicy meat patty with rich sauce over rice is a popular Hawaiian dish in Japan. I like demi-glace sauce, but you can replace it with any type of gravy you like. Choose minced meat that has some fat for a juicier patty.

SERVES 2

Canola oil for frying
Steamed rice 400 g (14 oz)
Eggs 2
Lettuce for garnishing
Cucumber for garnishing
Cherry tomatoes for garnishing
HAMBURGER PATTIES
Yellow onion $^1/_2$, peeled and chopped
Milk 1 Tbsp
Panko or dry breadcrumbs 1 Tbsp
Minced pork 100 g ($3^1/_2$ oz)
Minced beef 100 g ($3^1/_2$ oz)
Garlic $^1/_2$ clove, peeled and grated
Egg $^1/_2$
Salt a pinch, or more to taste
Ground black pepper to taste
Plain (all-purpose) flour for dusting
SAUCE
Demi-glace sauce 150 ml (5 fl oz)
Tomato ketchup 1 Tbsp
Usukuchi soy sauce $^1/_2$ Tbsp
Sugar $^1/_2$ tsp
Unsalted butter 1 tsp
Salt to taste
Ground black pepper to taste

1. Prepare hamburger patties. Heat oil in a pan. Stir-fry onion over medium heat until half translucent. Leave to cool until lukewarm. Mix with milk and breadcrumbs. Let it sit for a few minutes.

2. Mix minced meats, garlic and egg with milk mixture. Season with salt and pepper. Knead well to incorporate. Shape 2 patties and dust evenly with flour.

3. Heat oil in a pan. Brown both sides of patties over medium-high heat.

4. Fill one-third of the pan with water. Cover with a lid. Lower to medium heat and cook until water has evaporated and patties are done. Remove from heat and set aside.

5. Wipe pan with paper towels. Bring all sauce ingredients to a boil, then simmer for 5 minutes over low heat. Season to taste with salt and pepper. Return patties to the pan and simmer for another 5 minutes. Place patties over rice and pour sauce on top.

6. Meanwhile, heat 2 tsp oil in another pan. Fry eggs to make sunny-side-ups. Place on top of hamburger patties.

7. Garnish with lettuce, cucumber and cherry tomatoes before serving.

Note: Demi-glace sauce is sold in tins at Japanese supermarkets.

Mixed Sashimi Don
Sashimi Chirashi Don

SERVES 2

Hot steamed rice 400 g (14 oz)

Toasted white sesame seeds (*iri goma*) 2 Tbsp

Assorted sashimi (salmon, squid or any fresh seafood) at least 200 g (7 oz)

Shiso leaves for flavouring and garnishing

Cucumber for garnishing

Sweet pickled ginger (*gari*) to taste

Sashimi soy sauce to taste

wasabi to taste

SUSHI VINEGAR

Grain vinegar (*kokumotsu su*) 1 Tbsp

Sea salt $1/8$ tsp

Johakuto sugar 2 tsp

If you have a few kinds of sashimi cuts available, this would be a quick but fancy dinner option.

1. Stir together all ingredients for sushi vinegar in a microwave-safe bowl. Heat in a microwave for 20 seconds, until salt and sugar have dissolved. Alternatively, heat over a stove. Pour over hot steamed rice. Scatter over sesame seeds and mix well. Leave to cool to room temperature.

2. Meanwhile, make shallow slits on one side of the squid. On a flat surface, place a shiso leaf onto the uncut side of the squid and roll into a cylinder, then cut into smaller rounds.

3. Arrange sashimi radially on top of rice. Garnish with cucumber and shiso leaves. Serve with pickled ginger, sashimi soy sauce and wasabi.

Soy-marinated Grilled Salmon Don
Sake no Tsuke Yaki Don

This is a simple meal that tastes as great as it looks. Grilled salmon does not need a lot of time and effort to prepare, and is a healthy flavourful dish that satisfies anytime.

SERVES 2

Sea salt 1/2 tsp

Salmon fillets 2, each about 150 g (5 1/3 oz)

Canola oil for greasing

Steamed rice 400 g (14 oz)

Grated radish (*daikon*) for garnishing

Shiso leaves for garnishing

Lemon slices for garnishing

Koikuchi soy sauce to taste

SOY MARINADE

Koikuchi soy sauce 2 Tbsp

Mirin 1 Tbsp

Sake 2 Tbsp

Lemon slices 2

1. Sprinkle sea salt all over salmon fillets. Leave for 30 minutes. Rinse away salt and pat dry with paper towels.

2. Mix soy marinade ingredients together. Leave salmon fillets to steep in soy marinade overnight.

3. Heat and grease grill. If you do not have a grill, use a non-stick frying pan lined with greased aluminum foil. Grill salmon fillets until done.

4. Place salmon fillets on rice. Garnish with grated radish, shiso leaves and lemon slices.

5. Serve with koikuchi soy sauce.

Tempura Don
Ten Don

A typical tempura dish consists of prawns and assorted vegetables. There are three key points to note for good crispy tempura: Do not stir the batter too much; the batter must be kept cold at all times; lastly, the oil temperature for deep-frying must be constant. You can use ready-made tempura flour, called *tempura ko*. Simply add water to it and it is ready for use. However, try this recipe for making your own batter if you can.

SERVES 2

King tiger prawns (shrimps) 6, shelled and deveined, tails intact

Small Japanese eggplant (brinjal / aubergine) 1/2, halved

Vegetable oil for deep frying

Shiitake mushrooms 2, cleaned and stems removed

Shiso leaves 2

Steamed rice 400 g (14 oz)

TEMPURA BATTER

Egg yolk 1

Iced water 150–180 ml (5–6 fl oz)

Plain (all-purpose) flour 100 g (3 1/2 oz), sifted and chilled + more for dusting

Bicarbonate of soda 2 pinches

TEMPURA SAUCE

Japanese stock (*dashi*) 100ml (3 1/3 fl oz)

Koikuchi soy sauce 2 Tbsp

Mirin 35 ml (1 1/5 fl oz)

Johakuto sugar 1/2 tsp

Bonito flakes (*katsuobushi*) 2 Tbsp

1. Trim away the tip of each prawn tail and force out moisture with the dull edge of a knife. Make about three shallow cuts across the underside of each prawn. Press the back of each prawn to straighten its body. Pat dry with paper towels.

2. Make several cuts at one end of each eggplant piece. Spread tasselled ends so that they fan out. Soak in cold water and pat dry with paper towels.

3. Prepare tempura batter. Mix egg yolk and and iced water in a bowl. Add flour and bicarbonate of soda. Stir lightly with chopsticks. Do not overbeat. Adjust flour and iced water amounts according to how thick you want the batter to be. Place batter in an iced water bath to keep it cold at all times.

4. Preheat vegetable oil to 170°C (338°F). Dust prawns, eggplant, mushrooms and shiso leaves with flour, then dip in batter and slide into hot oil. Ensure that the oil temperature stays constant throughout. Deep-fry until light golden. Remove from heat and leave on paper towels to drain off oil.

5. Meanwhile, heat all ingredients for tempura sauce, except bonito flakes, in a saucepan. Bring to a boil. Add bonito flakes and simmer over low heat for 5 minutes.

6. Serve tempura over rice with tempura sauce.

Leek and Salmon Don
Negi Sake Don

SERVES 2

Hot steamed rice 400 g (14 oz)

Japanese leek 10-cm (4-in) length, white part only, coarsely chopped

Salmon sashimi 140 g (5 oz)

Extra virgin olive oil 1¹/₂ Tbsp

Usukuchi soy sauce ¹/₂ Tbsp

Shiso leaves for garnishing

Shredded Japanese leek for garnishing

Sashimi soy sauce to taste

Wasabi ¹/₈ tsp

SUSHI VINEGAR

Grain vinegar (kokumotsu su) 1 Tbsp

Johakuto sugar 2 tsp

Sea salt ¹/₈ tsp

A flavourful meal that doesn't leave you feeling too full, this can be easily prepared with salmon sashimi and leek, flavoured with simple seasoning ingredients.

1. Stir together all ingredients for sushi vinegar in a microwave-safe bowl. Heat in a microwave for 20 seconds, until salt and sugar have dissolved. Alternatively, heat over a stove. Pour over hot steamed rice and stir to mix well. Leave to cool to room temperature.

2. Soak leek in water for 15 minutes. Drain and pat dry with paper towels.

3. Using a sharp chopping knife, chop sashimi into a paste. Stir in olive oil, usukuchi soy sauce and chopped leek. Mix well and scoop onto rice.

4. Garnish with shiso leaves and shredded leek.

5. Serve with sashimi soy sauce and wasabi.

Chicken Steak Don
Tori Tsukune Don

Plain (all-purpose) flour for dusting
Canola oil for frying
Steamed rice 400 g (14 oz)
Shiso leaves for garnishing
Japanese cucumber for garnishing
Chopped spring onions (scallions) for garnishing
Mixed chilli powder (*shichimi / nanami togarashi*) to taste
Japanese mayonnaise to taste
CHICKEN STEAK
Minced chicken 200 g (7 oz)
Yellow onion 1/4, grated and strained
Egg 1/4
Potato starch 1 Tbsp
Salt 1/8 tsp
Pepper to taste
Breadcrumbs 2 Tbsp
SAUCE
Koikuchi soy sauce 40 ml (1²/₅ fl oz)
Johakuto sugar 2 Tbsp
Mirin 20 ml (²/₃ fl oz)
Sake 20 ml (²/₃ fl oz)
Arrowroot powder (*kuzuko*) 1 tsp + 2 tsp water

Tori tsukune, or chicken patty, is a versatile ingredient that can be used to prepare anything from *yakitori* (grilled chicken) to juicy burgers. Here, it is part of a hearty meal with steaming white rice.

1. Prepare sauce. Pour koikuchi soy sauce, sugar, mirin and sake into a saucepan. Simmer until it reduces by two-thirds. Thicken with arrowroot powder mixture. Set aside.

2. Mix all ingredients for chicken steak. Mix well until sticky. Shape two round steaks from mixture and dust with flour.

3. Heat oil in a pan. Fry steaks over medium-high heat until they brown on both sides.

4. Fill one-third of the pan with water. Cover with a lid. Lower to medium heat and cook until water has evaporated and steaks are done.

5. Dip chicken steaks into the sauce and place on rice. Garnish with shiso leaves, cucumber and spring onions.

6. Serve with mixed chilli powder and mayonnaise.

Note: Arrowroot powder is a starch made from the arrowroot plant, and is used as a thickener in Japanese cooking. It can be substituted with corn flour (cornstarch) or potato starch on a one-to-one ratio. If substituting with plain (all-purpose) flour, add 2 Tbsp for every Tbsp of arrowroot powder.

BASIC RECIPES

Steamed White Rice
Gohan

Well-cooked rice should be moderately sticky and very shiny with a slight fragrance. A typical rice measuring cup can hold a volume of about 180 ml (6 fl oz), which is about 150 g ($5^1/_3$ oz) of rice. The ratio of rice to water should be 1:1.1 or 1:1.2.

SERVES 3

Rice 2 cups, about 300 g ($10^1/_2$ oz)
Water 2 cups (360 ml / 12 fl oz) +
35–70 ml ($1^1/_5$– $2^1/_3$ fl oz)

1. Wash rice in ample amount of water. Stir quickly and discard cloudy water immediately.

2. Mix rice well with the heel of your palm, making about 20 circular motions to scrub out the starch.

3. Add water and drain. Repeat until water runs clear.

4. Pour in at least 2 cups (360 ml / 12 fl oz) water. Add 35–70 ml ($1^1/_5$–$2^1/_3$ fl oz) more water, depending on how moist you like your rice to be. Let it stand for at least 30 minutes, ideally 1 hour, before steaming in rice cooker.

5. When rice is cooked, let it stand for 10–15 minutes before fluffing with a rice paddle.

Japanese Stock
Dashi

MAKES ABOUT 600 ML
(19 FL OZ) STOCK

Kelp (konbu) 1 sheet, about 4 x 4 cm (1³/₄ x 1³/₄ in)

Water 600 ml (19 fl oz)

Bonito flakes (*katsuobushi*) 5–10 g (¹/₆–¹/₃ oz)

A typical Japanese stock is made from dried fish flakes. Versatile and flavourful, *dashi* is used in soups and a variety of other dishes. This stock can be kept refrigerated for up to 5 days.

1. Wipe kelp with a clean damp cloth or paper towel. Soak in 500 ml (16 fl oz / 2 cups) water for at least 30 minutes.

2. Bring to a boil over medium heat. Remove kelp right before it comes to a boil, but contiue heating kelp stock.

3. When the stock comes to boil, skim off any impurities or scum that rise to the surface.

4. Add 50 ml (1²/₃ fl oz) water and bonito flakes. Remove from heat.

5. Add another 50 ml (1²/₃ fl oz) water and leave for 10 minutes.

6. Carefully strain the stock through a damp cloth or paper towel. Use immediately or leave to cool before refrigerating.

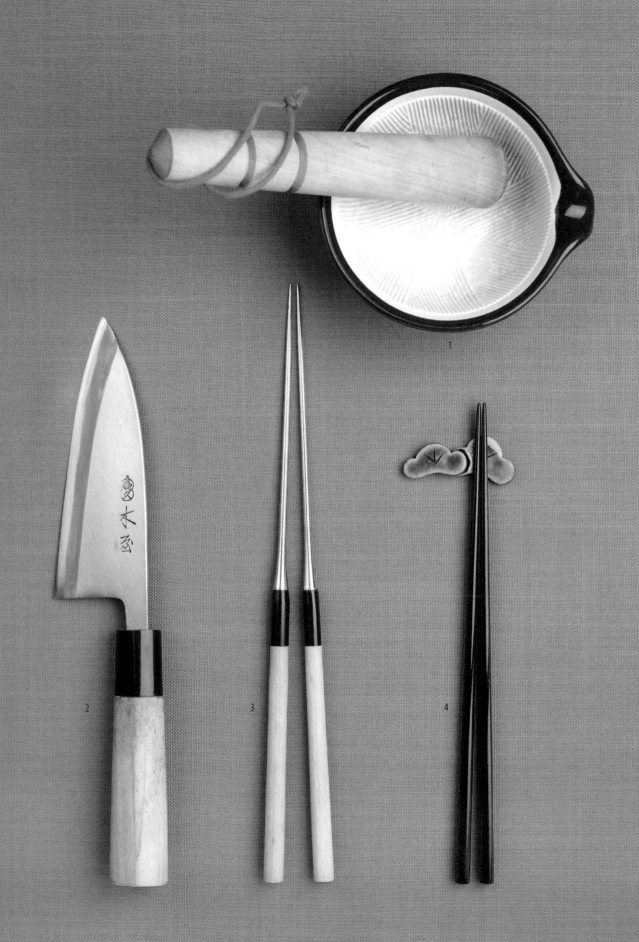

UTENSILS

1. **The Japanese mortar and pestle (*suribachi and surikogi* respectively)** are used to grind nuts and seeds or to create pastes, such as bean curd or fish paste. The mortar, or *suribachi*, is grooved on the inside to aid grinding. The pestle, or *surikogi*, is made of wood.

2. **The Japanese kitchen knife** has a blade on only one side (single bladed), and is made of steel. Shorter blades can be used to slice fish and cut through bone, while longer knives can be used to slice fish for sashimi. There are also knives that are made for cutting vegetables. Knives should be regularly maintained to ensure they are always in the best condition.

3. **Cooking chopsticks** are longer than those used for meals. Most are made from bamboo. The one pictured here are stainless steel chopsticks with sharp pointed ends, and used by professionals for plating purposes.

4. **Japanese chopsticks** are characterised by their pointed ends. When setting the table for a meal, the chopsticks should be placed directly in front of the diner with the pointed ends facing the left. Chopsticks are usually the only utensils provided for a meal, unless the food served is too soft to be picked up by chopsticks. Using other utensils with chopsticks is not considered appropriate table manners in Japanese culture. It is therefore important to take into account how food is prepared, and the ingredients or condiments should not be difficult to pick up with chopsticks.

5. ***Donburi* pan and lid** are mainly used to prepare *donburi* dishes with egg, such as oyako *don* and katsu *don*. The design of the pan, together with the help of a vertical handle, allows the cook to slide the food easily into a rice bowl. If unavailable, a small 15-cm (6-in) pan with a lid may be used instead.

6. **The traditional *donburi* bowl** comes with a lid and have a certain depth. Such a rice bowl should be able to hold enough rice as well as gravy or sauce. The *donburi* bowls used in this book can hold 180–375 ml (³/₄–1¹/₂ cups) worth of food. Other types of bowls, such as those that are used to serve nuts or café au lait may be used as well, as long as they are deep enough to hold a *donburi* meal.

5

6

GLOSSARY

1. **White radish (*daikon*)** is a root vegetable that is often used in Japanese cooking. When grating radish, note that the lower portion is spicier, and the top part sweeter. Grated radish aids digestion and is commonly served as an accompaniment to deep-fried dishes and grilled fish. The middle portion of a radish is said to be best used for simmering dishes.

2. **Japanese parsley (*mitsuba*)** belongs to the same family as coriander, and has a unique fragrance and a slightly bitter taste. It comes in clusters of three leaves, as the name *mitsuba* suggests. Both the leaves and stems can be used for cooking various dishes, such as chawanmushi (steamed egg custard), soups and salads.

3. **Shiso (*ohba*)** is a herb that is of the same family group as mint and basil. It is rich in carotene, vitamin B and dietary fibre. Shiso leaves can be either red or green, but green shiso is more commonly used. It is used in tempura dishes, sashimi and salads.

4. **Radish sprouts (*kaiware daikon*)** are usually grown hydroponically. It has an intense and pungent taste. Rich in folic acids and vitamins K, C and E, radish sprouts is a great ingredient for salads.

5. **Japanese leek (*negi*)** is used widely in Japanese cuisine. The white portion (*shiro negi*) is used for toppings and stews, while the green part is used to mask the strong smell of chicken flesh in soups.

6. **Japanese yam (*nagaimo / huai san*)** has thin beige skin and white sticky flesh. In Japanese cuisine, this is consumed raw, either grated or shredded. It is eaten as a salad mixed with soy sauce and poured over steamed rice or mixed in dipping sauce for noodles. Although it tastes excellent when cooked, the good enzymes in *nagaimo* will be destroyed by heat.

7. **Burdock (*gobo*)** is a vegetable with brown skin and has a unique earthy fragrance. It is a popular health food because it is rich in dietary fibre. Burdock can be used in various kinds of Japanese dishes such as stir-fries, soups, salads and deep-fried food. To prevent fresh burdock from turning brown, soak in water after peeling and cutting. To store, wrap with damp newspaper and refrigerate.

8. **Spicy cod roe (*karashi mentaiko*)** is cod fish roe marinated in chilli. It can be consumed raw with steamed white rice, as a filling for *onigiri* (Japanese rice balls) or as a pasta sauce. To store, wrap *mentaiko* in cling film and refrigerate. Note that it should be consumed within a month.

9. **Deep-fried bean curd puff (*aburaage*)** is softer and more moist than its counterpart in Chinese or South-east Asian cuisine. As it is hollow, *aburaage* can be used like a pouch to stuff meat or vegetables, and then stewed or pan-fried. Blanch in boiling water before use to remove excess oil.

10. **Dried radish (*kiriboshi daikon*)** has a slight pleasant crunch and is commonly used in Japanese braised dishes or salads. To name a few of its health benefits, it is rich in calcium, vitamin C and dietary fibre. Once the original packaging is opened, it is best to store in an air-tight container or resealable bag, and then refrigerated to prevent oxidation.

11. *Shibazuke* refers to **pickled vegetables**, which are usually made from cucumber or eggplant. It gets its pinkish colour from red shiso leaves, and has both sweet and sour flavours. It is served with plain steamed rice, but can also be used to flavour dips and sauces.

12. **Natto** are fermented soy beans, which may not be pleasant to those who are not used to Japanese cuisine because of its strong fermented smell and stickiness. However, many Japanese are addicted to its unique taste and texture. Natto is made from fermented cooked soy beans. It is typically taken with steam rice, mixed with soy sauce, chopped spring onions or fresh raw eggs. Natto is said to have great health benefits because it contains high-quality protein, enzymes and dietary fibre. It is also effective in preventing blood clots, high blood pressure and osteoporosis.

13. **Mixed chilli powder (*shichimi / nanami togarashi*)** (top) has a chilli powder base mixed with other spices such as sesame seeds, Japanese pepper and mandarin orange zest. *Shichimi* means "seven tastes", but there are actually more than seven ingredients used to create this spice mix. It is used to sprinkle over *donburi* dishes that have eggs, like oyako *don* and katsu *don*. **Japanese pepper spice (*sansyo / sansyo ko*)** (bottom) is ground dried pepper skin. It is sold in powder form, and has a spicy aroma and a pungent taste. *Sansyo* is used as a seasoning for eel or egg dishes as well as clear soups. Refrigerate after opening to retain flavour.

14. **Japanese mustard (*karashi*)** is sold either in powdered form or in a tube as a paste. The paste is ready for use while the powdered form needs to be mixed with water into a paste before using. Unlike western mustard, the base ingredient for Japanese mustard is not vinegar. It also has a stronger and more pungent taste. Japanese mustard can be used in salad dressings or as a condiment for deep-fried food and *oden* (winter stews).

15. **Johakuto sugar** is simply common white sugar used in Japan. It is more moist than other kinds of regular cane sugar, and dissolves even faster than castor sugar.

16. **Chicken bones soup granules (*torigara suupu no moto*)** is used for seasoning soups and other dishes. It has no additives so it is a preferred seasoning alternative. If unavailable, substitute with fresh chicken stock.

17. **Toasted sesame seeds (*iri goma*)** can be black or white. It is commonly used as garnishing and flavouring as it imparts a toasted fragrance to the dish.

18. **Tonkatsu sauce** (green bowl) **and Japanese worcestershire sauce** (brown bowl) are commonly referred to as *sosu* (derived from the English word "sauce") in Japan. *Sosu* can also refer to similar sauces that are vegetable-based and dark brown in colour. Tonkatsu sauce not only can be used for deep-fried pork cutlets (tonkatsu) and savoury pancakes (*okonomiyaki*), but also for sunny-side-up eggs, curries and stews.

19. **Grain vinegar (*kokumotsu su*)** is a sour seasoning brewed from grains such as corn, wheat or rice. It has a subtle taste so it complements the flavour of other ingredients without overpowering them. Grain vinegar is mainly used to make sushi vinegar, salad dressings and various marinades. There are other types of vinegars that have stronger aromas, such as rice vinegar and brown rice vinegar. They can be substitutes for grain vinegar.

20. **Sake** is rice wine made by brewing rice, malt and vinegar. There are many types of sake in Japan, but it is advisable to use sake made specially for cooking, and the dry type of sake for direct consumption. Sake is used to remove the strong smell of meat or fish. It can also add flavour to food.

21. **Mirin** is sweet rice wine made mainly from glutinous rice. Its sweetness is not from sugar but comes as a by-product of the brewing process. Mirin is used to naturally sweeten dishes as well as for glazing.

22. **White sesame paste (*neri goma*)** is a condiment which adds flavour to dips and sauces. Stir the paste very well before use as the oil and the paste will be separated if set aside for some time. Do not refrigerate or freeze. Instead, store in a cool shady place.

23. **Preserved squid (*ika no shiokara*)** is aged squid fermented in salt with all internal organs intact. It may be served with rice or even as it is with liquor. As a condiment, it can be mixed with blanched leafy vegetables as it lends more flavour to the dish due to its saltiness and rich ocean flavour.

Quantities for this book are given in Metric, Imperial and American (spoon) measures. Standard spoon and cup measurements used are: 1 tsp = 5 ml, 1 Tbsp = 15 ml, 1 cup = 250 ml. All measures are level unless otherwise stated.

LIQUID AND VOLUME MEASURES

Metric	Imperial	American
5 ml	$^1/_6$ fl oz	1 teaspoon
10 ml	$^1/_3$ fl oz	1 dessertspoon
15 ml	$^1/_2$ fl oz	1 tablespoon
60 ml	2 fl oz	$^1/_4$ cup (4 tablespoons)
85 ml	$2^1/_2$ fl oz	$^1/_3$ cup
90 ml	3 fl oz	$^3/_8$ cup (6 tablespoons)
125 ml	4 fl oz	$^1/_2$ cup
180 ml	6 fl oz	$^3/_4$ cup
250 ml	8 fl oz	1 cup
300 ml	10 fl oz ($^1/_2$ pint)	$1^1/_4$ cups
375 ml	12 fl oz	$1^1/_2$ cups
435 ml	14 fl oz	$1^3/_4$ cups
500 ml	16 fl oz	2 cups
625 ml	20 fl oz (1 pint)	$2^1/_2$ cups
750 ml	24 fl oz ($1^1/_5$ pints)	3 cups
1 litre	32 fl oz ($1^3/_5$ pints)	4 cups
1.25 litres	40 fl oz (2 pints)	5 cups
1.5 litres	48 fl oz ($2^2/_5$ pints)	6 cups
2.5 litres	80 fl oz (4 pints)	10 cups

DRY MEASURES

Metric	Imperial
30 grams	1 ounce
45 grams	$1^1/_2$ ounces
55 grams	2 ounces
70 grams	$2^1/_2$ ounces
85 grams	3 ounces
100 grams	$3^1/_2$ ounces
110 grams	4 ounces
125 grams	$4^1/_2$ ounces
140 grams	5 ounces
280 grams	10 ounces
450 grams	16 ounces (1 pound)
500 grams	1 pound, $1^1/_2$ ounces
700 grams	$1^1/_2$ pounds
800 grams	$1^1/_2$ pounds
1 kilogram	2 pounds, 3 ounces
1.5 kilograms	3 pounds, $4^1/_2$ ounces
2 kilograms	4 pounds, 6 ounces

OVEN TEMPERATURE

	°C	°F	Gas Regulo
Very slow	120	250	1
Slow	150	300	2
Moderately slow	160	325	3
Moderate	180	350	4
Moderately hot	190/200	375/400	5/6
Hot	210/220	410/425	6/7
Very hot	230	450	8
Super hot	250/290	475/550	9/10

LENGTH

Metric	Imperial
0.5 cm	$^1/_4$ inch
1 cm	$^1/_2$ inch
1.5 cm	$^3/_4$ inch
2.5 cm	1 inch